Sociological theory

Monographs in Social Theory

Editor: Arthur Brittan, *University of York*

Zygmunt Bauman   *Culture as Praxis*

Keith Dixon   *Sociological Theory*

Anthony D. Smith   *The Concept of Social Change*

A catalogue of the books in the *Monographs in Social Theory* series and in the other series of Social Science books published by Routledge & Kegan Paul will be found at the end of the volume.

Keith Dixon

Department of Sociology
University of York

Sociological theory
Pretence and possibility

Routledge & Kegan Paul
London and Boston

First published in 1973
by Routledge & Kegan Paul Ltd
Broadway House, 68–74 Carter Lane,
London EC4V 5EL and
9 Park Street,
Boston, Mass. 02108, USA
Printed in Great Britain by
Clarke, Doble & Brendon Ltd
Plymouth
© Keith Dixon, 1973
No part of this book may be reproduced in
any form without permission from the
publisher, except for the quotation of brief
passages in criticism

ISBN 0 7100 7601 0 (c)
     0 7100 7698 3 (p)
Library of Congress Catalog Card No. 73–75940

Contents

Sociology, a Scottish philosopher once remarked to me, is about what chaps do. I suppose not many practising sociologists would accept this statement in spite of the empirical spirit which informed it. Certainly, much sociological investigation is concerned to establish what men actually do in contrast to what they are popularly supposed to do. In an area where ignorance, prejudice and subjective judgment still hold sway over the public mind the sociologist is justly proud of his objective stance. Most sociologists are not content, however, with the role of mere 'fact-gatherer'. 'Brute' or 'piecemeal' empiricism is unfashionable. What confers professional prestige is explanation of human behaviour—couched in forms which bear *some* general resemblance to successful theorising in the physical sciences. Sociology is nothing, so it may be argued, if it is not a generalising science of human behaviour.

This book is concerned with an analysis of the status of the claim that sociology is, or ought to be, a theoretical science. My conclusion is not that such a claim is unfounded on *a priori* grounds but that it is formulated in such a way that a proper evaluation of its status is extremely difficult. Having, I hope, resolved some of these ambiguities, I conclude that the contingent objections to the possibility of sociological theorising are sufficiently strong for such activity to be labelled as pretence. Of course it is always possible by adopting a sufficiently broad and ambiguous definition of theory to rebut these contentions but linguistic sleight of hand, though it may lead to the disappearance of both critical distinctions and relevant objections, is still a conjuring trick.

Much of what I have to say is necessarily negative or destructive. But pretence to the theoretical is a hindrance to the development of sociology proper. It devalues significant empirical work by giving status to research findings only in so far as they relate to often arbitrarily conceived 'theoretical' concerns; it leads to a systematic neglect of the historical dimension in the explanation of human behaviour and it sets up ideals of explanation whose pursuit leads to sterility, frustration and even intellectual corruption.

The present climate of opinion in sociology is such that any attack on the possibility of 'theory' is liable to be seen as an attack on the possibility of sociology itself—a capitulation to the obscurantism of the romantic and the mystic. No one should read such implications into this work. In attacking the contingent possibility of theory I do not mean to devalue empirical expertise, analytic skill or the exercise of *disciplined* speculative intelligence. But intelligence can only flourish when released from the constraints of attempting to justify the unjustifiable.

Acknowledgments

I wish to express my thanks to the University of York and to my colleagues in the Department of Sociology for granting me paid leave of absence for the Michaelmas term 1971, and to the Department of Applied Economics and to University College, Cambridge, for providing an ideal working environment during my stay at Cambridge.

I am particularly indebted to Professor Ronald Atkinson and to Mr Arthur Brittan for their criticism and encouragement and to Alexander Stewart, Bob Blackburn and Ken Prandy of Cambridge for their often vigorous opposition to much that I have to say. I should also like to thank Dr Colin Campbell and Roland Hall of York and Anthony Giddens of Cambridge for commenting helpfully on various drafts or chapters of the book.

I am also indebted to those ladies both in Cambridge and York who were kind enough to offer secretarial assistance.

Finally I should like to express gratitude to Sandy and Frieda Stewart whose kindness made my stay at Cambridge very enjoyable and to my wife, Barbara, for enduring both my fits of depression about the book and my three months' absence from home.

K.D.

chapter 1

Ordinary language and theoretical explanations

.

ORDINARY LANGUAGE EXPLANATIONS

The description and explanation of human behaviour is not the prerogative solely of social scientists. Each of us is already equipped with a set or sets of concepts which enable us to make sense, more or less successfully, of our own behaviour and the behaviour of others. Explanations of human behaviour are given typically by referring to the motives, intentions and dispositions of people and to the reasons they have, or are alleged to have for their behaviour. Arguments frequently centre around the *evaluation* of the behaviour of others either in an attempt to elicit the meaning of actions or in making moral judgments about them. We ask questions about the significance of remarks, gestures and movements—attempting to see other people's behaviour and our own in terms of some consistent pattern which enables us to typify individuals and to simplify our relationships with them. In morally evaluating the acts of others we are interested in the question of whether they acted freely or under some kind of physical or psychological constraint. The states of affairs which people actively bring about are distinguished from things which happen to them and associated with, or parasitic upon this distinction are such notions as responsibility, culpability, justification and excuse.

In our accounts of human behaviour, explanation, description and evaluation interpenetrate such that apparently simple observations of a man's conduct become enmeshed within a complex of norms and values. To describe a man as cruel, for example, is to *evaluate* his behaviour and if it can be established that he acted under substantial constraint then our original description of his behaviour is significantly altered.

Typically, in our ordinary explanations of human behaviour, we form judgments against a background of 'acceptable' or accepted assumptions. It is assumed that deviations from certain norms of behaviour require special explanation. In Britain one does not require to explain why one drives on the left-hand side of the road; whereas leading a beribboned crab down the Strand might conceivably raise a few eyebrows. Furthermore, the mere act of labelling a man as deviant in some defined respects inclines us to see his behaviour under the description of that which requires special categories of explanation: a lie of a friend, for example, forces us to consider both the reasons for the lie and the motives of our friend; the lie of a 'confidence trickster' is already partially 'explained' through the attachment of that label.

Where the motives of others are intelligible to us in the sense of meeting our expectations, we tend to eschew the use of the words motive, intention and reason—for enquiries into motivation appear redundant in such circumstances. We typically query a man's motives when we suspect that the reasons he gives for his behaviour are not the real reasons.[1] Nevertheless, the fact that in ordinary usage we tend to restrict the use of the words motive, intention and the like to deviant, suspect or puzzling aspects of behaviour does not entail the presumption that 'motive' cannot operate as an explanatory term in a wide range of 'normal' human behaviour for in such cases a person's motives are well undestood but left implicit in giving an account of his behaviour.

Such explanatory or descriptive categories as motive, reason, disposition or proneness, intention, voluntariness, involuntariness, constraint and cause are, of course, used normally to answer very *specific* enquiries about a man's behaviour within a well-understood context. As J. O. Urmson points out,[2] when puzzled by a man's behaviour, we tend to ask general questions like: 'What led him to do that?', 'What was his reason for doing that?', 'What possessed him to do that?', rather than to ask for explanations couched in 'causal' terms. But even in the use of such terms as 'possessed', 'led', 'his reason' and the like, there exist pre-formulated favoured types of explanation. To ask the question about a man, 'What possessed him to resign his job?', is to imply that *his* stated reasons were, in some sense, unsatisfactory or that no *good* reasons for his actions were apparent to the enquirer. An answer to such a question might in fact involve a rejection of the original formulation of the question, i.e. 'nothing "possessed" him to resign; he was unhappy and had managed to get something better.'

The usefulness of our everyday accounts of human behaviour depends upon what we are prepared to accept as explanation. At perhaps the 'lowest' level we might be prepared to accept dispositional accounts of a person's behaviour, e.g. 'Why was he so rude to me?'; 'Oh, don't mind him, he's always aggressive'. In this example, an 'explanation' is desired merely to reassure one party to a conversation that he has said nothing specific to offend. If the relationship specified is transitory or unimportant then this explanation would normally suffice. Should a deeper relationship be presupposed one might expect a corresponding interest at a deeper level in explaining the behaviour of a friend who is prone to aggressiveness. A psychiatrist or close friend, for example, might wish to examine a very wide range of possible explanations for a man's habitual aggressiveness which would take into account, either as complementary or exclusive, varieties of explanations—the man's motives and reasons, and other psychological or social constraints which appeared to be impelling him towards this form of behaviour.

Now such 'everyday' explanations of human behaviour, although sociologically interesting in that their analysis may reveal a fascinating complex of 'background expectancies' relevant to our judgment of others, are in an important sense non-theoretical. That is, the generalities implicit in everyday explanations of behaviour do not necessarily cohere within some *system* of explanation. Rather, there is a closer analogy with proverbial or gnomic wisdom which offers a series of tenuously related aphorisms as a guide to explanation and judgment.

One does not refer to a set of 'covering laws' which hold for a particular range of human behaviour in explaining, say, the lie of a friend. Nor does one typically formulate general hypotheses which are put to the test of falsification. One refers doubts about the behaviour of a friend not to a set of axioms, nor to some variation of an S-R model of behaviour but to the minutiae of the situation. The questions are, rather: how am I to interpret this particular action in this set of circumstances; does the response of others to one's own actions fit into a pattern consistent with already-formulated expectations; is the behaviour serious or the product of a mere mood of frivolity or cynicism? And so on.

In such situations, of course, I have available to me a number of possible interpretations of the given behaviour based upon my past experience and the recorded or unrecorded experience of others. I may have encountered similar situations before, read about them in novels or had them recited to me by friends. But only in the loosest possible of senses can I be said to be *theorising* about the matter in hand. What I am interested in is the explanation of a specific response set in a particular context, and it would be a very foolish thing to generalise from a manifold of particular personal experiences (except perhaps in a tentatively inductive sense relevant to the necessity to make an immediate practical decision). Indeed we define the socially obtuse as those who are inclined to make too facile an extrapolation of their own limited insights.

The difficulty about relating sociological explanation to common sense or even historical accounts of behaviour is the widespread disagreement amongst professional sociologists as to the nature of their discipline. I want to direct my arguments, however, to a broad spectrum of practitioners who would agree that, at the very least, sociology is a *generalising* science of human behaviour—however the terms 'generalising' and 'science' are to be defined. But in order to avoid the kind of primitive, subjective *generalities* already implicit in folk-lore, sociology needs an inter-subjectively defined basis upon which *generalisations* can be properly secured. This 'basis' is notoriously difficult to locate. In empirically testing, for example, the proposition that 'too many cooks spoil the broth' it is perhaps not sufficient to confine oneself to 'cooks', 'broth' and the interpretation of 'ego and alters' response to 'tasting-situations'. Nor is a simple stochastic proposition correlating the number of cooks with the quantity of spoiled broth sufficient. For broth-making is merely one activity of man—an activity which is differently conceived, interpreted, enacted and justified in different circumstances. One man's broth is another man's poison.

What is required then, it has been argued, as the preliminary to any generalising science whatsoever is some concept, or set of concepts, which gives anchorage to widely different forms of behaviour. Distinctively theoretical explanation needs, it is alleged, to relate to data which are unambiguous and which can be consistently defined. One has to treat data as having some common basis such that one can move from the interpretation of one specific action or event to another via a complex chain of theoretical reasoning. In our every-day usage, we take for granted existing categories of classification and explanation simply because we tend to use them on a specific, even an *ad hoc*, basis to meet the contingencies of practical living. But in aiming at a theoretical explanation of behaviour one cannot be content with the *ad hoc*. The notion of a *systematic* understanding of behaviour must begin, it has been suggested, with an ordering or an analysis of 'the given' in its most fundamental aspect.[3]

THE CONSTRUCTION OF A DATA-LANGUAGE: BEHAVIOURISM

One possible way of locating a data-base is to attempt to construct a *language* which embodies only the unambiguously given elements in human behaviour. A data-language is defined as 'that language which is used to describe the evidence adduced in support of a theory'.[4] The requirements of such a language are strict. It must be 'neutral' with respect to existing theories, new theories and to the value judgments of any (social) scientist; it must refer only to precise and measurable observations. Attempts to construct data-languages have had a chequered history but I want to concentrate upon the version of this positivist doctrine which has been especially influential in the social sciences—namely behaviourism.

Anyone embarking upon however limited a discussion of behaviourism faces the problem that for some sociologists the very label conjures up the notion of redundant stimulus–response models which by ignoring the dimension of the subjective meaning attached to behaviour by 'actors' systematically distort the explanations of human behaviour; whilst for others the label 'behavioural' is a defining characteristic of the discipline which marks it off from 'speculative', 'intuitive' or 'empathetic' accounts of the way men behave.

One can, however, make a simple distinction between a 'behavioural science' and 'behaviourism' as a methodology. In its widest connotation the word 'behavioural' simply marks off overt behaviour either from processes which occur in the central nervous system or more generally from the notion of inner states. A 'behavioural scientist' as such makes no explicit or implicit recommendations or judgments as to the relationship or lack of relationship between what goes on in the organism and what is manifested publicly. Behaviourism strictly interpreted is a very different kettle of fish.

Central to traditional accounts of behaviourism is the belief that concepts of mind, purpose and subjective meaning are capable either of being reduced to a set of observation statements or of being dismissed as wraith-like entities and hence without counterparts in the 'real' world. The relegation of subjective factors to a methodologically irrelevant 'black-box' confirms for the 'philosophical behaviourist' their dubious existential status. Thus the description of the world in terms of a neutral, uninterpreted language of observation-statements is a complete description. Speculation on what lies 'behind' overt behaviour (except neurophysiological and internal chemical states of the physical organism) is beside the point. Such speculations are 'metaphysical reifications' or theoretical constructs which not only go beyond the evidence but cannot attach to it. This most general form of behaviourism has been distinguished however from the 'more careful methodological' formulation of behaviourism in the current psychological literature. As I. E. Farber notes:[5] 'To the best of my knowledge no one these days denies the existence of mental events.' Watson did so on occasions but Farber condemns this view as 'silly'. For Farber, 'mental events exist and in a commonsense way we know what we mean when we refer to them' but it is unnecessary, he argues, to appeal to such events in a 'thoroughgoing account of behaviour'. Indeed mental events may be analysed simply in terms of 'behavioural, physiological and environmental items'.

Ernest Nagel[6] also argues that much of the criticism of behaviourism is directed towards a caricature of that approach. He claims that the behaviourist can recognise the existence of 'directly experienced' and 'private' psychic states but argues that these states are 'adjectival or adverbial' of bodies having certain types of organisation rather than 'entities' inhabitating those bodies. However we are meant to interpret this metaphorical account of the mental, Nagel makes it quite clear that 'psychic states' are in his view *always* accompanied by 'certain overt and publicly observable behaviours of that body'. Such overt behaviours constitute, according to him, 'a sufficient basis for grounding conclusions about *the entire range* of human experience'. He writes: 'a behaviourist can maintain without inconsistency that there are indeed such things as private psychic states and also that the controlled study of overt behaviour is nevertheless the only sound procedure for achieving reliable knowledge concerning individual and social action . . .' It is difficult to see what difference the 'concessions' made by both Farber and Nagel concerning the existence of mental events make to the traditional version of behaviourism. One could of course readily conceive of a programme of investigation which contained a built-in methodological assumption that the only possible objects of study in the human sciences were 'overt and publicly observable behaviours' but neither Farber nor Nagel appear to limit themselves to this position. It is not the case for them that we are (unhappily or necessarily?) *restricted* to an examination of overt behaviour. Quite the contrary. The behaviourist programme is conceived of as wholly appropriate to an investigation of the 'entire range of human experience'. All that can meaningfully be said in explanations of human behaviour can be couched in the language of observation statements. The analysis of brain states together with overt behaviour (including verbal reports) is sufficient unto itself and although the existence of mental events is not specifically denied they are redundant in any thorough-going explanatory scheme. Thus the distinction between 'philosophical' and 'methodological' behaviourism (a valid distinction in its own right) breaks down if one examines the practices and writings of most behaviourists.

There are, then, good grounds for treating behaviourism as a distinctively metaphysical doctrine—but it is a doctrine conceived as a response to alternative metaphysics of behaviour which allow a central place to the *a priori* and the teleological in the explanation of behaviour. Behaviourism is, in effect, one form of a rejection of an entire philosophical tradition—that of Cartesian dualism—the doctrine that mental phenomena and overt behaviour are irreducibly different sorts of things.[7] In opposition to Cartesianism behaviourism leans heavily upon traditional empiricist accounts of the world which seek to establish an indubitable empirical base as the ground of all knowledge. Designated observables, logically primitive and 'uncontaminated' by concepts, are regarded as preconditions for the avoidance of the abyss of philosophical rationalism, *a priorism* and metaphysical speculation in general.

The objections to Cartesian dualism are of course well known. Feigl has written of the existence of so-called laws governing mentalistic phenomena as 'nomological danglers' which violate the principles of scientific enquiry[8] whilst Ryle's[9] contention that Cartesianism is inconsistent with the plain facts that we can determine what people think and feel even better than themselves certainly points up a crucial weakness in the Cartesian position. But perhaps the most damaging criticism of Cartesianism and one seized upon by behaviourists relates to the fundamental unintelligibility, or at least lack of communicability, of the necessarily private world of mental events envisaged in that view. The description of these allegedly private mental events without reference to a public language which assumed behavioural criteria as constituting mental phenomena was held to be impossible.[10]

Indeed, behaviourism may be considered as a specific response to that traditional *reductio ad absurdum* of philosophical theories—solipsism. The argument that since it is not possible to apprehend another person's sensations directly it follows that there is no method of inferring what they are, or even that they occur, is a familiar one in philosophy.[11] The unpalatable consequence of such extreme scepticism, based upon an analysis of particular observations of particular perceptual events by 'isolated' individuals, are notorious. At worst they involve the dissolution of the external world and the consequent invalidation of scientific procedure based upon the assumption of an empirical bedrock. Philosophical behaviourists have taken these arguments seriously enough to cause them to assert that introspectable events are capable of being reduced to overt, publicly-accessible behaviour.

The central problem for the behaviourist, however, is how to locate and describe data in terms which avoid reference to 'private' Cartesian mental entities. The selection of certain data-statements as 'basic' to explanation needs to be justified. Traditionally this justification has involved taking perceptual experience, analysed as primitive and incorrigible sense-data, as brute fact. But this traditional empiricist move will not do for the behaviourist. Perceptual *experience* cannot be taken to be the brute facts upon which theory operates simply because 'experience' can be construed as essentially private and beyond the reach of a behavioural science. What the behaviourist needs in his construction of data-language is some concept of a datum which eliminates all reference to postulated inner states.

The simplest propositions within the behaviourist's explanatory scheme are thus expressions of elementary behavioural *discriminations* for if such discriminations are taken to be the immediately given then they are to be established publicly on the basis of experimental investigation; whether a man can discriminate between event 'A' and event 'B' is, for the behaviourists, a matter which may be publicly settled without reference to any notions of 'inner states' or 'perceptual experiences' which remain beyond the scope of scientific enquiry. Elementary discriminations between types of behaviour or events in the world are *not* to be taken as 'indicators' of private mental experiences. They are themselves the bedrock of inquiry.

Karl Popper,[12] however, argues that the behaviourist programme is invalidated in principle since the concept of a theoretically unsullied elementary discrimination has no application. He writes: 'Every description uses universal names (or symbols, or ideas): *every statement has the character of a theory: or an hypothesis:* The statement, "here is a glass of water" cannot be verified by observational experience. The reason is that universals which appear in it cannot be correlated with any specific sense experience.'

Popper, as is well known, in fact rejects the whole reductionist approach in favour of asking the question 'What kind of deductive consequences can we select for the purpose of testing scientific hypotheses?' Empirical statements in science he sees as statements made in indissoluble connection with theory. The search for a language of *basic* statements which somehow 'reflects' or describes 'immediate experience' he rejects as not contributing to clarity. The only empirically basic statements which Popper will allow are 'singular existential statements' which we simply 'decide to accept' on the basis of a consensus of scientists. What determines the usefulness of an empirical statement is its function within the theoretical scheme—as a potential falsifier of theory. 'Theory', concludes Popper, 'dominates the experimental work from its initial planning up to the finishing touches in the laboratory'—and decisions as to the validity of a given theory rest upon the analogy of a verdict given by a jury rather than by a reference to our perceptual experience. He writes:

> The empirical basis of objective science has thus nothing 'absolute' about it. Science does not rest upon rock-bottom. The bold structure of its theories rises, as it were, above a swamp. It is like a

building erected on piles. The piles are driven down from above into the swamp, but not down to any natural or 'given' base; and when we cease our attempts to drive our piles into a deeper layer, it is not because we have reached firm ground. We simply stop when we are satisfied that they are firm enough to carry the structure, at least for the time being.

Popper seems to be making two logically independent points here. First, that a theoretical structure does not rest, proven absolutely as it were, upon a bedrock of indisputable or 'brute' fact, and second, that any view based upon the reduction of data to observation statements, protocol sentences, atomic propositions or the like is invalid. Now if Popper is right, there may appear to be a sense in which the selection of explanatory categories is arbitrary—their selection may seem at least as arbitrary as the choosing or 'plumping' for fundamental moral categories or principles. But this selection clearly cannot be made without reference to some 'ultimate' point of anchorage in the brute world. The whole tenor of Popper's work carries the implication that the existence of an empirical bedrock is a necessary condition of scientific theorising even if the location and description of such bedrock raises insoluble philosophical difficulties.

The rejection of the behaviourist conception of a data-language does not thereby commit one to an abandonment of empirical enquiry. All data, whether in the natural or social sciences, it may be argued, must necessarily be viewed through the lens of theory or accumulated together with a series of background assumptions which render the data less than neutral either in an explanatory or in a value sense. Neither events in the physical world nor human behaviour can be viewed as 'brute facts' in some absolute sense of those words. Nevertheless, in theoretical activity one is forced to treat some data as 'harder' than others and it is this judgment as to what data is to be deemed 'hard' that enables theorists to erect a series of empirical trip-wires. It is my contention that the possibility of treating data as 'hard' almost always depends upon the prior existence of a *well-founded and established theoretical framework*—a touchstone theory. There is usually a *reciprocal* link between theory and data—the data being as 'hard' as the theoretical structure permits; the theory being possible only if one can establish hard data.

Now scientific advance depends not so much upon the collection of an array of relcalcitrant observations as upon imaginative reconceptualisations such as Einstein's clarification of the concept of 'simultaneity' in his exposition of relativity theory. Nevertheless 'hard data' are often required to trigger off such reconceptualisations. Let me now elaborate this point by an analysis of a fundamental change which occurred within physics during the early part of the twentieth century.

Two 'small dark clouds' appeared on the horizon of classical physics at this time—the negative results of the Michelson-Morley experiment and the so-called ultra-violet catastrophe of the Rayleigh-Jeans law. As an illustration of the theory-data relationship, one need only consider the latter case.[13]

Briefly, it was discovered that the predictions from classical theory of the *intensity* of the 'black-body' radiations in relation to the *wave length* of the radiations emitted was contrary to experimental results.

Thus, one might draw two graphs to illustrate the point.

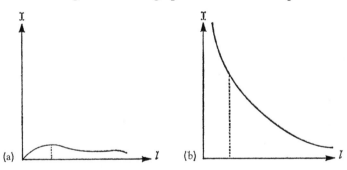

Figure 1

(a) represents the distribution of intensity (I) of light of different wavelengths l emitted by a black body as found experimentally.

(b) represents the distribution of intensity (I) of light of different wavelengths l emitted by a black body on theoretical grounds (Rayleigh and Jeans law, based upon the Maxwell-Lorentz electro-magnetic theory, Newtonian mechanics and Boltzman's statistical theorem).

In the theoretical case, (b), the intensity is greatest at very short wavelengths (i.e. the ultra-violet region), in clear contradiction to the experimental data. The two curves, however, were similar for high values of l. Not only was there no empirical agreement but the theoretical conclusions were literally absurd since they imply that the radiation inside the 'box' would have to be infinite.

In December 1900 Max Planck put before the Academy of Sciences in Berlin his fourteenth memoir on black-body theory, in which he formulated a new concept—the quantum hypothesis—which solved the black-body problem. Catastrophe had been averted.

Thus, classical physical theory foundered upon the twin factors of incoherence and lack of empirical fit—the existence of hard data inconsistent with the established body of theory proving the direct incentive towards a reconceptualisation of the theory.

The anomalies involved in the 'ultra-violet catastrophe' problem could not have been conceived, however, had it not been for the existence of a prior theoretical framework which identified the crucial nature of the problem. Nor could the theory have been challenged without 'a bedrock of fact'. But such a 'bedrock' was only so-called after the event. A clash between experimental data and theoretical considerations in the physical sciences does not always lead to a rejection or modification of the existing body of theory. Sometimes the theory is so powerful that the experimental data is held to be dubious or simply an unhappy anomaly—a dark cloud.

Thus, the idea that one can operate in scientific terms with two levels of language—a formal theoretical language and a data-language linked by rules of correspondence—appears inadequate to meet the subtle interplay of theory and data. The separation of theory and data can only lead to a distortion of what occurs in the development of a science.

The relationship between theory and data which I have been discussing holds only for a *successful* theoretical science.[14] Neglect of this distinction leads to an improper inference on the part of many social scientists that all data is *theoretically* interpreted—the social theorist's task being to elaborate his theories in such a way as to change our 'orientation towards the facts'. Now whilst it is clearly true to say that a putative 'observational' statement in the physical sciences is already highly interpreted in theoretical terms, this is not necessarily the case in the social sciences simply because there are no overall 'touchstone' theories whose component theoretical sentences can be treated to all intents and purposes as sentences expressing hard data. The gap between theory and data in the social sciences makes the behaviourist notion of the separation of theoretical and data-languages look much more plausible at first glance. The location of 'brute' social data, however, involves another kind of difficulty. Social data is interpreted not theoretically but within a framework of culturally understood *meanings* which make nonsense of the behaviourists claim that an uninterpreted observational language is possible. Consider for example the attempts at operational definition of concepts like marital maladjustment. Clearly there are no touchstone theories of marital maladjustment whose general acceptance would permit one to regard the phenomenon as an intelligible datum within a complex theoretical system. Marital maladjustment is in a fundamental sense a 'fact of *life*' embedded within a whole set of norms and background expectancies which give sense to the concept. Operationally to define the concept it would be absurd to undertake an atomistic analysis of normative discriminations (if indeed that phrase makes sense) and characteristically sociologists have not attempted to investigate the phenomenon by reducing the concept to a set of elementary discriminations. Kirkpatrick,[15] for example, operationally defines marital maladjustment as 'that quality in a marriage which causes a close friend to classify the marriage as maladjusted'—encapsulating the assumption that a close friend is able to *interpret* the behaviour of the couple. There is of course nothing wrong with this procedure provided that it is acknowledged that the problem of interpretation is pushed back one stage from the concern of the investigator to the concern of other participant observers. Clearly it may prove to be the case that such an operational definition 'works' in practice. Other 'variables' may be discovered which correlate highly with estimates by close friends that certain marriages exhibit 'maladjustment'. Nevertheless, such discoveries rest upon the assumption that behaviour is interpreted according to a culturally-specific set of meanings and expectations. Such operational definitions are neither data-statements in the behaviourist's sense nor are they theoretically-loaded data in the sense discussed in relation to the physical sciences.

I have argued, then, that the attempt to construct a neutral data-base which will operate as a foundation for theory is in principle not possible. In any case successful theoretical sciences do not as a matter of fact reflect this separation between theory and 'hard data'. Two main alternatives are now left open to the sociologist or psychologist who wishes to claim that his explanations are superior to those typically employed in common usage: that is, he must give an account of the relationship between theory and data which is not subject to damaging criticism at the epistemological level or he must point to the possibility of establishing as a data-base an *already* '*interpreted*' language—the language of 'action'. I shall return to the second of these alternatives in a later chapter but I want now to direct attention towards the first problem—that which relates to the logic of successful theorising.

THE LOGIC OF SUCCESSFUL THEORY

The hallmark of a good theory, it has been suggested, is that it specifies the conditions under which it may be discarded for a better one. I may, for example, hold that all human behaviour may be understood if it is recognised that men act solely and always out of self-interest. There are at least three ways in which I may respond to a challenge to this 'theoretical' proposition. If faced with a counter-example of alleged human altruism I may (a) accept the counter-example and abandon or modify my belief; (b) attempt to *interpret* the alleged counter-example as one consistent with my theory; (c) deny the counter-example on empirical grounds. Now if the counter-example cited is one of heroic self-sacrifice, I can hardly resort to empirical denial. I might, however, seek to redescribe the act of self-sacrifice as essentially self-interested. If, however, I responded in this way to *all* possible counter-examples, I would have implicitly denied the very possibility of the falsification of my belief and this would render it useless for the purposes of explanation.

Now this view of the central importance of the possibility of falsification as a defining characteristic of theory has had, under the influence of Popper and his disciples, a profound effect upon social scientists. Much writing on the methodology of the social sciences refers explicitly to the hypothetico-deductive model of theory and very many research papers are written up in a style consistent with this view of theory. The notion is that uninhibited speculation needs to be followed up by rigorous testing techniques which lead either to conclusive refutations or to an array of confirmations which reinforce the probable truth of the theory. Nowhere in this naive falsificationist doctrine (one, incidentally, which Popper never held) better illustrated than in A. L. Stinchcombe's *Constructing Social Theories*.[16]

I want to use Stinchcombe's analysis as a point of departure for considering both the *objections* to naive falsification and more sophisticated versions of that doctrine.

Much of Stinchcombe's book is interesting and can be made methodologically defensible but his core recommendations are suspect. He writes: 'Our purpose has not been to outline the ultimate justification of scientific belief but to outline how scientific belief systems operate in practical fact so that we can use this knowledge in constructing social theories' (p. 56).

But in fact, as I shall show, his approach is both *a prioristic* and dogmatic. The hypothetico-deductive model operates, according to Stinchcombe in the following way, in the following situations:

Situation I

Theory A implies Fact B
B *is false*
∴ Theory A is false

Situation II

A implies B
B *is true*
∴ A is more credible

Situation III

A implies $B_1 B_2 B_3 \ldots B_n$
$B_1 B_2 B_3 \ldots B_n$ false
∴ A is false

Situation IV

A implies $B_1 B_2 B_3 \ldots B_n$
$B_1 B_2 B_3 \ldots B_n$ true
∴ A substantially more credible

He writes that the canons of logic demand that we *reject* a theory if it implies something that is false—a very stringent requirement indeed!

If confronted with a 'very large number of possible theories' we select the best theories, according to Stinchcombe, by a process of deduction and testing which eliminates alternative theories. What is of relevance in this procedure is the devising of so-called 'crucial experiments'. Thus:

Situation V

Possible theoretical candidates are:
A or C or (D, E . . .)
(D, E . . . unlikely)
A *implies* B_1
C implies (not B_1)

But B_1 true
$\therefore$ C false (and D, E ... unlikely)
$\therefore$ A very much more credible

The practical examples used to illustrate this procedure are drawn from Durkheim's *Suicide*.

Let me now examine two of the central tenets of Stinchcombe's version of the hypothetico-deductive method. He argues:

(a) that we must reject a theory if it (deductively) implies something that is false;
(b) that we choose between theories on the basis of conducting crucial experiments.

The first requirement, as I have mentioned, is impossibly stringent. One or more repeatable recalcitrant observations simply do not necessarily overturn a good theory. A theory which incorporates the virtues of parsimony, predictive strength and high-level explanatory power with respect to a wide range of empirical data is not eliminated or rejected by anomalous facts. Rather, as Lakatos puts it,[17] their existence merely increases the 'problem tension' within the body of theory or such facts are simply regarded as 'monsters' or 'dark clouds'. One hopes that with the further elaboration of the theory, the monster will turn into a mouse and the clouds will disappear. But it is not sufficient merely to assert that in fact no scientist actually operates with the naive falsificationist doctrine expounded by Stinchcombe. There are good logical reasons for not so doing.

Lakatos regards the central fallacy of naive falsification as being the tendency to set up what he calls the 'mono-theoretical' model of criticism. On this model 'one *single* theory is confronted by potential falsifiers supplied by some authoritative scientist'. But typically the situation is that, at least in the physical sciences, theories are also involved in the experimental techniques used to uncover facts —the Doppler effect with the consequent red-shift of light from distant galaxies, for example, is a theoretical position which is taken as crucial in the determination and interpretation of stellar phenomena.

Falsification and rejection may occur in the cases where observations repudiate a *high-grade* conjunction of statements in the hierarchy of an already suspect theory when an alternative theory is already in an embryonic state—but such cases are rare indeed in the history of science. Naive falsificationism makes the mistake of assuming that at the point of crisis science is divided into two areas —the problematic and the unproblematic, theory and brute data. Now as I have argued previously, in any sophisticated science, the relation between theory and data cannot be represented in this simple-minded fashion for in cases of conflict between different theories or between theory and theoretically-loaded observation, one has to make a judgment as to which is to be regarded as problematic and which unproblematic. One's touchstone is not always the data : but as Lakatos notes : [18]

> The problem is then *not* when we should stick to a 'theory' in face of the 'known facts' and when the other way around. The problem is not what to do when theories 'clash with facts'. Such a 'clash' is only suggested by the mono-theoretical deductive models. Whether a proposition is a fact or a theory depends on our methodological decision . . . the problem is which theory to consider as the interpretative one which provides the 'hard' facts and which the explanatory one which 'tentatively' explains them . . . we propose a maze of theories and Nature may shout . . . (not NO) . . . but INCONSISTENT.

From Lakatos's acute analysis it can be seen why naive falsification looks so good to the social scientist. For typically the sociologist is faced either with a 'theory' (or a set of speculations) which is consistent with a very wide range of empirical affairs—in which case the 'rigour of falsificationism' looks promising—or he is faced with very simple, low-level propositions which he can test against what he treats as brute descriptions of the world. In the latter case, what he is doing, however, looks less like 'testing a hypothesis' than collecting data for the establishment of a low-level empirical generalisation—a rather different and less sophisticated kettle of fish.

The arguments propounded above also tell against the equally naive notion that we can choose between theories by conducting 'crucial experiments' which are identifiable *in advance*. For science progresses by a series of research programmes in which confirmatory experiments build up over time to support theories at varying levels of generality and explanatory power. It is only when 'problem-tension' becomes acute that experimental results begin to look as if they are *crucial* to the holding of a given theory. Thus a series of inter-related experiments might be seen *with hindsight* as crucial in the overthrow of a given theory, but at the time of its imminent overthrow it cannot be unambiguously asserted that any body of theoretically interpreted or 'hard data' is crucial. Resistance to the implications of so-called crucial experiments may be fully engendered by dogmatic adherence to the *status quo* but resistance may also be construed legitimately (*as it turned out*) as a proper response in the defence of a well-articulated established theory of considerable power.

There are, however, more fundamental objections to the whole notion that any formal criterion will serve to enable one to discard particular scientific theories. D. W. Peetz,[19] for example, asserts that our search for a formal criterion exhibits 'a misplaced craving for generality'. 'We are bewitched', he writes, 'by what we call "The Scientific Method"', but in fact the methodologies of science are open-textured, he alleges, 'and bear only a "family resemblance" to one another'. Laws of nature are to be construed on an analogy with verdicts arrived at in a court of law where what is relevant is the particular context in which a judgment is given.

Peetz's conclusions are, however, premature. He bases his argument on the inadequacies of both justification and naive falsification as formal criteria—leaping to a neo-Wittgensteinian conclusion on negative evidence. A more radical approach—that taken by Thomas Kuhn—is to accept Peetz's conclusions but reinforce them by giving an account of changes in the theoretical structure of science which rests upon extra-logical considerations. That is, the rejection or acceptance of scientific theories are made dependent not upon the application of formal logical criteria but upon socio-psychological considerations.

Kuhn's celebrated *The Structure of Scientific Revolutions*[20] marks a radical alteration of emphasis in both the philosophy and sociology of science. Mannheim, for example, in his *Essays in the Sociology of Knowledge* (1952), had explicitly ruled out 'logico-mathematical' and natural scientific knowledge from the area designated as the Sociology of Knowledge. Logic, mathematics, and science were for Mannheim free from the taint of ideology—the possibility of establishing objective formal criteria for the acceptance or rejection of scientific theories was acknowledged.

Kuhn both challenges this assumption and applies his conclusions to the traditional distinctions employed in the philosophy of science. He argues, for example, that the 'influential contemporary distinction between "the context of discovery" and "context of justification" seems extraordinarily problematic' when one examines actual situations in which knowledge is gained. Terms like 'consensus', 'authority', 'dogma', 'faith', 'conversion' and 'gestalt-switch' replace the traditional arsenal of formal dichotomies in the philosophy of science.

Kuhn argues that what he calls 'normal science' is carried on under the auspices of some 'paradigm' which is more or less universally accepted by competent scientists. Normal science consists in 'puzzle-solving' within the bounds of the accepted paradigm. Where change occurs, whole paradigms which are historically discrete and logically incompatible are overturned through a gradual shift in the consensus of informed scientific opinion. The success of new paradigms or theories is often only demonstrated after a 'gestalt-switch' on the part of scientists—justifications for change in logical terms, he implies, are given after the event.

He writes (p. 24): 'As in political revolutions, there is no standard higher than the assent of the relevant community.' Of the function of argument in the process of changing consensus, he remarks:

> This is not to suggest that new paradigms triumph ultimately through some mystical aesthetic. On the contary, very few men desert a tradition for these reasons alone . . . because scientists are reasonable men, one or another argument will ultimately persuade many of them. But there is no single argument that can or should persuade them all. Rather than a single group conversion, what occurs is an increasing shift in the distribution of professional allegiances.

The man who resists this shift, however, is not to be conceived of as 'illogical' for 'the man who continues to resist after his whole profession has been converted has *ipso facto* ceased to be a scientist'.

As Kuhn acknowledges in his 1970 postscript and elsewhere, the use of the term paradigm is not unambiguous. A paradigm is both 'the entire constellation of beliefs, values, techniques and so on, shared by the members of a given community'—which defines presumably what it is to be a scientist—and also those theoretical and experimental orientations shared by practitioners of a 'scientific speciality' which enables research workers to concentrate upon fruitful 'puzzle-solving'.

But within this second category exist paradigms particular to individual sub-disciplines within science. The scientific world may thus be conceived of as consisting of areas of consensus at decreasing levels of generality which permit, in terms of these paradigms, *non-controversial* research to continue as the main plank of scientific activity. Where theoretical or experimental anomalies occur, these are tolerated until a 'gestalt-switch' occurs within the particular scientific community concerned.

Now clearly as an analysis of the relation of societal or group pressures upon the development of science, Kuhn's arguments are interesting and informative, but the claim made by Kuhn is imperialist. He explicitly asserts that there is 'no systematic decision procedure which properly applied must lead each individual in the group to the same decision. In this sense it is the community of specialists rather than its individual members that makes the effective decision', and again : 'The conversion experience that I have likened to a gestalt-switch remains therefore *at the heart* of the revolutionary process. Good reasons for choice provide motives for conversion and a climate in which it is more likely to occur' (my italics).

It is difficult to interpret these passages as anything else but a claim to the logical priority of changes in *authoritative consensus* in determining *scientific* change. Kuhn strenuously denies, however, the charges of Watkins and others that his approach equates science with theology or is essentially irrational. But it is difficult to see how Kuhn can escape from the dilemma that scientific change occurs either on the basis of the rational resolution of 'problem-tensions' or it occurs as a socio-psychological response by the scientific community as a consequence of a relatively sudden and irrational shift in authoritative scientific opinion.

Of course, a growing sense of problem-tension, a generalised dissatisfaction with particular theories, may lead to a process of rationally-induced change of opinion within a discipline or a scientific community at large. Further, no one denies the possibility that rational changes in theory may be delayed, often for long periods, by the authority structure within the scientific community—as Lakatos remarks: 'Kuhn certainly showed that psychology of science can reveal important and indeed sad, truths.'[21]

But Kuhn's use of the terms 'conversion', 'faith', and the like go beyond the approach which distinguishes carefully between the ideology of scientists as a community and scientific knowledge itself. A scientist is a member of a number of different worlds in which it is possible to respond 'rationally'. As a member of a scientific community, for example, he is subject to many kinds of pressures to conform to the 'paradigms' of his day. When he deviates from the 'shared cognitive culture' of science or from specific sub-disciplinary expectations, he needs to show success or at least its distinct possibility. But he is also a member of what Popper has called the 'third world' of ideas, and to ignore the rational basis of a scientist's participation in this third world is to discredit science by an illegitimate reductionist move which treats men as responding merely to social pressures.

We cannot rest content with either Peetzian neo-Wittgensteinian evasion nor Kuhnian socio-psychologistic irrationalism. But is there an alternative, more sophisticated philosophy of science which takes into account both the *tenor* of Kuhn's objections and the deficiencies of naive falsification? I think there is. Or rather the possibility of establishing such has been indicated quite precisely.[22]

What characterises the physical sciences is their *successful growth* —a growth which is dependent upon the *fecundity* of the theories which are developed. As Lakatos notes: 'A theory is better than its rival if it has more *empirical content*, that is, if it forbids more observable states of affairs and if some of this excess content is corroborated—that is, if the theory produces novel facts.'[23]

A series of successive theories, each of which satisfies these two requirements, generates a 'progressive problem-shift'—that is, they offer an increasing possibility for the resolution of both 'puzzles' (in the Kuhnian sense) and anomalies. Theories which do not satisfy these requirements are, on the contrary, soon worked out—they lead only to semantic or linguistic disputes. Thus Kuhn's notion of 'normal science' can be reinterpreted to refer to the acceptance by the scientific community of programmes of research which lead to progressive rather than degenerative problem shifts. Clearly all 'progressive' theories will incorporate anomalies or 'dark clouds' but typically, *in the absence of better theories*, these anomalies will be tolerated if the current paradigm is successful in resolving real problems. Revolutions occur in science only when a particular theory begins to show a degenerating problem shift and alternative theories are available which look promising enough to handle the range of difficulties encountered in 'normal' research activities. Lakatos distinguishes two types of interdependent research programmes in this connection: a 'negative heuristic' programme which protects the 'hard core' of a theory by digesting anomalies, and a 'positive heuristic' programme which seeks continually to confirm, develop, or falsify those variants in the protective belt around the 'hard core' theory. Thus Lakatos argues: 'we may appraise research programmes, even after their "elimination" for their heuristic power: how many new facts they produced, how great was their capacity to explain their refutation in the course of their growth.'

Thus, the successful growth of science is defined as the ability over time to produce theories which lead to progressive problem shifts. The procedures for testing such theories are not *simply* falsificationist but repeatable; numerous falsifications are relevant to the strength of either the 'hard core' theory or its 'protective belt' and will lead eventually to the construction of alternative theories and research programmes.

Lakatos cites many examples of progressive problem shifts in the history of the physical sciences. The classic case, he argues, is Newton's theory of gravitation. When first produced 'it was submerged in an ocean of anomalies and opposed by the observational theories supporting these anomalies'. Nevertheless, over time the theory transformed these counter-examples into corroborating instances and predicted new theoretical difficulties which were resolved through a continuing research programme. Newtonian physics in its early formulations led, Lakatos argues, to predictions which ran counter to current observational theories, but such was the strength of the 'hard core' theory that apparent 'refutations' were transformed into confirmations via a reinterpretation of existing 'observational theory'. Not only were novel facts adduced by the theory and anomalies resolved, but the very data of physics were reinterpreted in the light of the theory. The pay-off from so powerful a theory was such that it led to a series of research programmes which were so consistently successful that Newtonian theory became entrenched over time as a 'paradigm'. The success of Newtonian physics was dependent not so much upon a shift of community allegiance, but upon the possibilities it opened up for consistent theoretical and empirical growth.

Lakatos's analysis of the growth of the physical sciences through the logic of progressive problem shifts, however, leaves a fundamental problem unresolved.

The issue may perhaps be best illustrated in diagrammatic form (Diagram 1).

Early 'paradigm' (1)	Crisis period		Later 'paradigm' (2)
	Problem of the explanation of TENACITY		
Well-founded body of theories giving progressive problem shifts but tolerating anomalies. SMF applies.	(1) Problem tension (Old theories still adhered to).	(2) Possible resolution of problem tensions (New theories in embryonic form).	New paradigm —shifting the perspective of earlier theories or replacing them with new fundamental concepts. Progressive problem shifts apparent. SMF applies.

Diagram 1

In cases (1) and (2) there are few problems about maintaining the criteria of sophisticated methodological falsificationism (SMF). In both cases the adherence to the paradigm is fully explained by the fact that it leads to successful growth in terms of puzzle-solving. Problems occur, however, at the immediate point of crisis where increasing anomalies both at the theoretical and the empirical level create problem tensions which are seen to be irresolvable within the current paradigm. The hardcore of (1) appears to be threatened. Attempts to resolve this problem tension may lead to the emergence of new theories and concepts which successfully explain key anomalies. These new theoretical perspectives may then be generalised so as to reinterpret both existing theories and theoretically-loaded observations. What is unexplained in Lakatos's analysis is on what logical grounds different groups of scientists adhere to the old and new perspectives respectively. It cannot be the case that the 'revolutionaries' have clear-cut logical grounds for believing that the new paradigm will lead to progressive problem shifts since, as Lakatos himself points out, until the traditional 'observational theory' has been radically reinterpreted, the likelihood is that the new perspectives will issue in 'refutations'. These may later be 'turned into corroborating instances' if the theory is powerful and successful, but there can be no guarantee *at the time of crisis* that this happy state of affairs will come to prevail.

At crisis points in the history of science then it may appear that a Kuhnian analysis in terms of the operation of non-logical shifts of allegiances amongst scientists might be appropriate. For where there are no *compelling* reasons to accept either the old or the new, the *tenacity* with which individual scientists adhere to one or the other 'paradigm' is likely to be a function of their temperament, their ties with other scientists and their psychological attachment to their own insights.

Now, two observations need to be made in this context: first, the fact that scientists may appear to act primarily from socio-psychological motives when faced with scientific *dilemmas* in no way goes to show that the progress of science as a whole or even over time in a period of crisis is governed by non-rational processes; and second, it might well prove feasible, by examining cases where a suggested new paradigm or theory has *failed*, to demonstrate that there are in fact both good and bad *reasons* for adhering to certain paradigms even at times of crisis. At such times it might prove, for example, that the *elegance* of new mathematical techniques might be a decisive and rational criterion in the assessment of one's theoretical allegiances, or it might be shown that there were good logical reasons for defending and elaborating a new paradigm, even if in the last analysis it proved sterile.

However this may be, Kuhn's resort to a wholly externalised account of the development of successful theorising can only be viewed either as a challenge to locate and elaborate the logical criteria involved in such development, or as an appropriate account of *deviations from the logical norm*. Whatever the evaluation by contemporary biologists of Lysenko's theories, for example, there is no doubt that, at the time they were devised, only the ideological pressures of the Soviet establishment permitted their grudging acceptance and development as 'paradigms' in Soviet biology. Kuhn's social-psychologism is a 'last-resort' analysis of the problems involved in successful theorising, but the fact that its challenge has not been fully met does not justify one in clutching its dogmatic scepticism to one's breast.

Sophisticated methodological falsificationism may not prove to be the final answer to the logic of the sciences but one cannot, except in one's most sceptical hour, doubt that philosophers of science have improved upon both Baconian inductivism and Carnapian positivism. If then sociologists are misled into attempting to match the 'paradigm of the physical scientist' it is important that they become more sophisticated in the philosophy of science. But, of course, the scientistically-inclined sociologist faces even more fundamental problems than those involved in the Popper-Kuhn-Hanson controversies.[24] For he is faced with difficulties whose solution is thought to be *logically prior* to the debate about falsification.

chapter 2

Matching the physical science paradigm

An acquaintance with the literature of sociological theory in general clearly reveals that, judged by the standards of the natural sciences, theory construction in sociology lacks a coherent rationale. There is widespread disagreement not only about the methods of social enquiry but about the nature of the discipline itself, the role of ideological commitment and the nature of human action. Sociology, it could be argued, is still, in spite of its century of relative academic respectability, in a 'pre-paradigmatic' stage: that is, there exists no accepted paradigm for 'professional practice'. As a consequence one would expect there to be a proliferation of competing 'theories' and associated research programmes running alongside relatively straight-forward empirically-based projects of an essentially descriptive nature. This is indeed the case. No one theoretical perspective has achieved dominance and professional recognition simply because no single theoretical focus has been able to sustain a progressive problem shift over time. The reasons for this cannot any longer be attributed to the alleged 'infancy' of sociology, for theoretical infancy is in fact *defined* by that pre-paradigmatic state already referred to. The 'infancy hypothesis' explains nothing: it merely points to a state of affairs.

Sociologists, however, are usually unwilling to accept that their discipline is in a fundamental sense non-theoretical; they want to establish that sociological theorising is validated as an activity in-dependently of a natural-science based 'scientific method'. In this, however, they are often curiously ambivalent.

Roland Robertson, for example, in *The Sociological Interpretation of Religion* writes: 'the reader should not be led to anticipate a theory or set of theories organised upon the ideal lines of the philosophy of science . . . much of what is of interest to the sociologist of religion remains unamenable to highly rigorous and analytic treatment.'[1]

Yet later in the same work there occurs the following: 'One would expect that ethical and psychic deprivations would tend to attract individuals to gnostic types of belief . . . however such suggestions are not intended as *genuine hypotheses*' (my italics).

What is the force of the word 'genuine' here unless to make a distinction between merely plausible speculation and hypotheses which may be rigorously tested according to criteria of the kind drawn from successful theoretical sciences? There seems to exist within even relatively eclectic sociological theorists some internal mental device which enables them to hold simultaneously both that sociological theory is plausible speculation and that it is capable of formulating hypotheses which may be rigorously tested in empirical terms.

Of course, there is clear sense in which plausible speculation cannot be carried out without close reference to the empirical; but the claim that sociology is a 'theoretical science' involves more than this. It demands that the relationship between conjecture and refutation be specified in a certain way rather than being left open to individual interpretation.

A greater difficulty in establishing theories which lead to progressive problem shifts, however, is the inability of sociologists to handle the so-called 'causal problem'. This inability may stem from at least two different sets of problems. First, there is the general issue of whether it is meaningful to talk of human action at the individual or social level as being 'caused'. May the description and explanation of human behaviour not require the use of a language of 'intentions' rather than 'cause'? Second, there is the issue of whether the contingent *complexity* of human actions defeats causal analysis.

In speaking of the latter problem, Robertson writes, with respect to Weber's Protestant Ethic:[2]

Generally speaking, the major problem apart from the sheer complexity and, we suggest, the ultimate *unanswerability* of the Weber hypothesis, is that variables [sic] like religious culture and economic growth . . . vary in their nature of association from societal context to societal context. This problem of *contextual uniqueness* is undoubtedly the most confounding one in the general problem area (my italics).

This is not *a priori* comment from an historian or philosopher but the considered opinion of someone immersed in a 'theoretical' research area. I want to suggest that if, on examination, theoretical problems of this kind are seen to be 'unanswerable', and if in fact problems of 'contextual uniqueness' prove 'confounding' one needs to look very closely at the ambitions of the theorist in posing the problems, that is, at the very nature of the questions themselves.

In ordinary usage the word 'cause' is invariably employed against a background of a standing set of complex initial circumstances (designated 'conditions'). What is to count as a 'condition' and what a 'cause' is often dependent on the practical interests of the investigator. Thus an enquiry into a car accident by an insurance company focuses upon those elements in a situation which indicate possible negligence on the part of the driver as well as the mechanical state of the vehicle, the road conditions, the density of the traffic *et alia*. Such usages of the word 'cause' are invariably context-specific. We ask why *this* particular car under *these* particular circumstances was involved in an accident in this particular place and at this time. Sometimes, as in referring to drunkenness or speed as a 'cause' of accidents, certain 'general causal factors' are hinted at, but such general statements are nowhere near as stringent in their application as the statements of necessary and sufficient conditions held to be characteristic of the mathematically expressed laws of physics.

In general in the analysis of human action as in the physical sciences, however, we may want to say 'A caused B' if and only if instances of 'a' causing 'b' occur in a wide range of relevantly similar circumstances. But the central issue is what is to count as 'relevantly similar circumstances'. Such circumstances are assessed as relevant either because of certain practical interests which we have in ascribing *responsibility* for actions (as in the accident example); but more ambitiously, because we have available a background of theoretical considerations (a set of interconnected confirmed hypotheses) whereby we assess, prior to further experimental testing, which of the variables amongst the set of standing initial conditions is likely to qualify as causal. Such theoretical assumptions are then tested or re-tested by controlled experimentation, perhaps according to the classic formula of Mill's method of Agreement and Difference.

Now it is a trite observation that both these methods of assessment of causal relevance involve difficulties for the social scientist, for unless he abandons his pretensions to generality, he cannot be content with the loosely-knit practically-biased judgments involved in common usage nor can he hope presently to match the theoretical sophistication and degree of experimental control of the physicists. The problems of 'compound causality' (causal factors), multiple causation (causal over-determination) and the mutual dependency and interaction of causal variables are no mere abstractions to the practising social scientist. As MacIver has demonstrated, research in the general area of deviant behaviour has in the past thrown up a wide range of 'causally unsatisfactory' explanations including 'single determinant' theories, 'broadly inclusive condition or trend' theories, 'single factor' theories, 'assortment of heterogeneous factors' theories and mere statements of statistical correlation backed by plausible interpretations. The contingent difficulties of matching what is alleged to be the causal paradigm of the physical sciences have led many sociologists, especially under the influence of the neo-Humean attack on the whole notion of causality as a productive agency, to propose different ways of handling explanations of human behaviour.

Characteristic of this change in emphasis has been the resurrection of organic or 'systems' models of human behaviour in which reference to causal factors is, so it is alleged, redundant. But alongside such models, which characteristically employ concepts of equilibrium, homeostasis and the like, there exist even more general theoretical perspectives which seek: (a) a 'tentative resolution' of the 'conflict-consensus' debate; (b) to express sociological propositions in law-like form—social variables being linked by causal relationships which may be classified on a scale from hard to soft; or (c) to express 'quasi-causal' relationships between such 'gross variables' as 'culture and the economy'. It is difficult to write of such pseudoscience with even the appearance of patient enquiry. Nevertheless, in what follows I hope to demonstrate that whatever the difficulties in establishing causal accounts of human behaviour at the *individual* level the sociologist interested in a macroscience of human behaviour is faced with problems of such enormity that philosophers of science have hardly dared enter the field—or perhaps they have thought it scarcely worthwhile. What follows then is a frontal attack on macrosociological theory. Much of the criticism I have to make has been taken note of in the past, but it has been accepted as criticism of a *particular* mode or school of theory. What I contend is that all so-called 'macrotheories' in sociology are likely to prove implausible and pseudoscientific simply because they are a series of different responses to questions which are at the moment and for the foreseeable future beyond our conceptual and intellectual resources. Let me begin then by illustrating this thesis from the history of the development of the concept of equilibrium. Such concepts have by now been elaborated into a 'science of macrocybernetics' but I think that my readers may find Pareto and Parsons enough for the immediate purpose.

(i) Equilibrium models

In the natural sciences, the notion of forces operating within a closed system so as to maintain that system in a steady state suggests stable or unstable mechanical systems within the field of statics. But dynamical processes also exhibit equilibrium given changes in certain key variables within the system. In the various forms of equilibrium whether mechanical, thermodynamic, chemical or homeostatic the energy exchanges which take place are assumed to take place in a *closed* system. In the reversible chemical equilibrium for example:

$$4H_2O + 3Fe \rightleftharpoons Fe_3O_4 + 4H_2$$

a state of equilibrium is maintained by physically isolating the system from the influence of other variables which would effect the reaction. In mathematical formulations of thermodynamic equilibria the relations between variables are deduced by a process of abstraction rather than physical isolation—the abstracted theory of equilibrium then being applied as an 'idealisation' to appropriate phenomena which exhibit an empirical approximation to the idealised set of conditions. Thus the concept of equilibrium is necessarily associated with the concept of a closed system whose variables stand in a determinate relation to one another, whether this system is empirically isolated or theoretically constructed.

Before examining the special use of equilibrium—that of homeostasis—which has been particularly influential in the social sciences, I want to examine the application of the concept of broadly mechanical equilibrium to the social sciences. Vilfredo Pareto[3] serves as a classical example of a man, trained in the mechanical sciences, who later turned the conceptual armoury of mechanics to sociology. Not surprisingly, Pareto's contribution to sociological theory tended to exhibit crude positivism although his mathematical training enabled him to distinguish clearly his own constructed 'systematic' theory from the empirical social world.

Pareto's sociological theories may be viewed from a methodological point of view as exhibiting three main components. First, an assumption is made that societies are in a state of mechanical equilibrium in which each of the discrete parts of the system stand together in a state of mutual independence: 'like so many little bits of lead attached by elastic threads which interlace in a thousand ways. You cannot move one of these pieces of lead without altering the form of the system.'[4] Second, in reaction to his own previous liberal, rational and anti-interventionist views, Pareto came to believe that, as Finer puts it: 'The bulk of human activity is not due to rational processes at all but to sentiments; men feel an urge to act, then invent justifications afterwards.'[5] Third, he held that although social facts were external to the observer theoretical systems were not to be regarded as reflections of reality but as constructs of the human intelligence which were relevant only in so far as they enabled men to formulate the (disconfirmable) laws of social interaction.

All forms of social life, according to Pareto, depend upon the factors which determine the alternation of élites. The Paretian model deliberately excludes large elements of reality, and concentrates upon a definition of equilibrium which narrowly restricts the variables which are held to define any state of equilibrium. The model operates with the concept of negative feedback in that if any part of the system 'is artificially subject to modification different from the modification it undergoes normally, a reaction at once takes place tending to restore it to a normal state.'[6] Societies are to be studied, however, not as entities in a state of dynamic equilibrium but as a series of static equilibria. Although societies may change continuously the only possible methodological approach for the sociologist is to study social change via a comparison between models of society which remain theoretically static but at different points of equilibrium at different points in time.

Society as a whole is determined for Pareto by the totality of forces influencing it, but: 'The state of a *concrete*⁷ equilibrium in a given society is a product of all these effects, actions, and reactions. In this it *differs* from a state of *theoretical* equilibrium obtained by considering one or more of the elements . . . instead of all of them.' The selection of the fundamental variables which govern a state of equilibrium involves then a recognised and necessary theoretical distortion of social reality.

A social system for Pareto is defined in terms of the operation of at least three interdependent variables subsumed under the categories of logical and non-logical action—that is, those of residues, derivations, and interests—and a further variable, that of a tendency to social stratification and circulation of power based upon 'natural' inequalities of talent and personality amongst men. External factors may limit what is possible for any social system but they do not limit its internal operation. The 'validity' of such models is determined both by their internal consistency and their empirical fit. The aim of a scientific sociology implicit in Pareto's work is the progressive refinement of theoretical models of social systems in order to gain a more exact understanding of social behaviour. It is necessary to use this 'systems' approach, according to Pareto, in sociological investigation precisely because single-law uniformities are contingently difficult to discover in the social sciences. He writes: ⁸

For us, therefore, scientific laws are nothing other than experimental uniformities. In this respect, there is no difference whatever between the laws of political economy or sociology and the laws of other sciences. Such differences as there are between them are of quite another kind subsisting mainly in the *varying degrees to which the effects of the various laws intertwine* . . . in some cases, the intertwining is so complicated that it is difficult to disentangle the effects. Such cases crop up in biology, geology and especially in meteorology. It is with these latter sciences that the social sciences are most closely related.

Furthermore, Pareto notes, 'experimentation as distinct from observation is not readily available to the sociologist for whom the main difficulty lies precisely in finding ways for unravelling this tangled skein produced by the intertwining of many different (exceptionless) uniformities.'

The statement of this methodological problem seen from one vantage point could hardly be bettered. It remains at issue, however, whether a systems approach is best fitted to achieve the object of unravelling the tangled causal skein. Pareto's scheme has the virtue that his 'variables' are limited in number; he is not content with a generalised concept of the interdependence of unknown parameters, as a *theoretical* construct. But his selection of a limited number of variables poses in an acute form the dilemma for the 'systems' theorist whose choice of theoretical constructs appears to lie between a system that restricts the number of variables so as to parody social reality or to extend the range of variables to such an extent that the system becomes useless as an explanatory construct. That Pareto is clearly impaled upon one horn of this dilemma will, I hope, become apparent from a more detailed examination of his system.

Absolutely basic to Pareto's concept of social system is his distinction between logical and non-logical action. Logical actions are defined by Pareto as those which are 'logically linked to an end, not only in respect to the person performing them, but also to those other people who have more extensive knowledge; that is to say . . . behaviour which is subjectively and objectively logical in the sense here indicated. Other actions we shall call non-logical.'

'The criteria as to what is logical and what is non-logical is a comparison', writes Finer, '. . . between the ends–means relationship as seen by the performer and as seen by the observer. Where

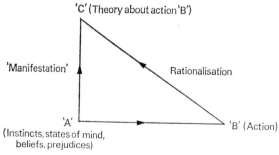

Figure 2

the two correspond, the action is logical.' The category 'non-logical' is a residual one into which Pareto consigns all actions not consistent with this definition. Most human action, Pareto argues, in fact is determined 'non-logically'. Cognition and rational explanation of action occur predominantly after the event as a form of rationalisation. Figure 2 shows a diagrammatic representation neatly expressing Pareto's theory of non-logical action.

Non-rational beliefs, prejudice and the like ('A') are for Pareto 'the true element of social equilibrium'. They are, by and large, 'the true causes' of human action. A reason for action, however, can operate as a cause of behaviour but only if the action is 'logical' in the defined sense. In most cases, theories about actions are the 'direct' manifestation of irrational beliefs—'theories are masks'.

'We are shown a curved mirror; our problem is to discover the form of the object so distorted.' The 'residues', the non-logical basis for human actions, however, are not to be identified in the Paretian scheme with the psychological concept of 'instincts', 'drives' or the like, though Pareto uses the term 'instinct' on occasions to refer to residues. Residues are those constant elements as used in a theoretical explanation or justification of any human act. Thus, although sexual appetite is not in itself a residue, it may be treated as such in so far as it gives rise to theories (of ascetism, say) about human behaviour. Freudian psychology, although Pareto was ignorant of it, might well be regarded as an exercise in the exploration of such 'residual' explanation of human action in so far as sexual appetite and its distortion was the common feature used in the explanation of a variety of psychological and social theories about man's actions. Residues, when present in explanation, as a matter of analytic necessity give rise to 'derivations' (or rationalisations) or human actions. In logical action, the term 'residue' is inappropriate according to the Paretian scheme and is replaced by the term 'interests'.

Interests are 'material wants' in so far as they give rise to logical (means–end) reasoning. The satisfaction of basic human desires for food, shelter, warmth and the rest may be typically regarded as logical actions. The two analytically-connected terms 'residue-derivation' in the non-logical sphere of conduct are thus matched by the notion of 'interest' alone in the logical sphere. Members of the ruling élite dominated by the so-called Class I residues are more likely to adopt a 'naked' (i.e. self-conscious) self-interest policy than those possessing the more traditionally-orientated Class II residues. Thus élite rule tends to be more openly 'logical' (i.e. self-interested) in the former case than in the latter. Conservative, bureaucratic and paternalistic élites will tend, according to Pareto, to act 'self-interestedly' whilst disguising the fact from themselves and others by a series of 'derivations', clothing their true interests by a theoretical or moral cloak. 'Interest' or 'residues' may thus have the same empirical referent. What is crucial is whether 'interest' is consciously recognised. If it is, then the action is logical; if not, then the action is non-logical.

It is not my intention in this thesis to examine the irritatingly crude conceptions of the nature of political action and human psychology, exhibited by Pareto in this scheme. Any conceptual scheme which aims at adequate explanations must satisfy the criteria of both internal coherences and empirical fit. Obviously, much of Pareto's simple-minded writing on the typology of social groups which rests on an equally dubious hypothesis that differences in 'natural endowment' will be more or less reflected in social stratification has been superseded. The crudely empiricist tenor of his writing as reflected by his division of human actions into logical and non-logical categories together with his own primitive (i.e. pre-*Language, Truth and Logic*) version of a verification principle does, however, give rise to doubts about the coherence of his own system.

Any system can maintain the characteristic of internal coherence provided it defines its terms of reference on a strictly analytic base. Clearly, had Pareto maintained the view that *all* human action was non-logical in character, his 'system' would have been less open to attack but even more empirically limited than it already is. The introduction of the concept of logical (or rational) action as a possibility for man drives a wedge into the basic conceptual scheme. The wedge is assimilated into the system through a strict empiricist definition of logicality which cuts off a limited area of human conduct—that of conscious pursuance of the 'scientific' means to a consciously formulated end, generally self-interest—as being unproblematic and hence of little sociological interest. The question to be raised is whether such a criterion adequately defines the field of the rational in human thought and action and whether indeed the criterion of logicality itself, as used by Pareto, is consistent with his own work.

Peter Winch has attacked Pareto's distinction on the grounds both of its positivistic overtones and its internal incoherence. Winch argues that the residual nature of the category non-logical will lead to assimilation of types of human behaviour which are altogether dissimilar. In particular, he concentrates upon Pareto's treatment of the Christian custom of Baptism. Holding, as he does, that all forms of religious activity are non-scientific, and hence non-logical, Pareto argues that religious rites have as a common element the notion of purification (whether by blood, water, etc.), the symbolic cleansing of the individual of a sense of guilt. The end product of these rites—the alleged restoration of individual integrity—is due to a 'vague feeling that water somehow cleanses moral as well as material pollution—and from this "residue" numerous derivations arise which constitute differences in "theology" '. Winch objects to this procedure in that it 'rejects as nugatory whole classes of reasoning within an accepted class . . . ideas cannot be torn out of their context . . . It is nonsensical to take several systems of ideas to find an element in each which can be expressed in the same verbal form and then to claim to have discovered an idea which is common to all systems.' Pareto's account of Christian Baptism is akin in Winch's eyes 'to observing that both the Aristotelian and Galilean system of mechanics use a notion of force and conclude that they therefore make use of the same system'.

Now Winch's comments clearly do expose weaknesses in Pareto's scheme in that there occurs in his categorisation of human behaviour into logical and non-logical actions an undiscussed premiss that science and only science (in the wide sense employed by Pareto) is a form of logical behaviour. Religious activity together with morals and aesthetics is relegated to a category of the non-logical which, Winch argues, is used in a pejorative sense. The non-logical, in spite of Pareto's protests to the contrary, does appear to be equated with the illogical and what is illogical must necessarily be either a mistake in an essentially logical process, which when subjected to correction will be recognised as such, or a 'rationalisation' based upon false beliefs. Pareto clearly recognises religion as falling into the second category. Hence his desire to explain away religious experience by seeking a common element in all religious experiences.

Where Winch is correct in his critical attack is not, it seems to me, in his basic contention that 'forms of life' and spheres of discourse have their own unassailable logic[9] but that Pareto's account of the sociology of religion is wholly inadequate. All religious activity arises in differing complex social situations and the form of (as well as the motivation towards) such activity may vary in a similarly complex fashion. Of course, if religious activity is to be regarded as empirically falsifiable, or confirmable, or given through modes of knowledge other than the empirical then another dimension of explanation is required in explaining its persistence. That Pareto thought of religion as well as moral ideals in politics as so much 'mystification' (to use the fashionable Marxian phraseology) is apparent. On these grounds, he may well be criticised as taking too much for granted. But surely it is not the case as Winch appears to maintain that 'explaining away' religious activity may be ruled out upon *a priori* grounds?

It seems to me that some kind of distinction between rational and non-rational action needs to be made in attempting to elucidate and explain human behaviour, although clearly Pareto's distinction is not adequate to his task since it rules out possible autonomous areas of discourse as 'derivative' without proper consideration of the issues involved. Clearly the means–ends schema propounded by Pareto need not exhaust all meanings of the word 'rational'. The answer to the question 'What ought I to do?', for example, lends itself to rational enquiry which goes beyond consideration of the technical problem of the relation of means to ends.

Pareto's scheme of explanation of human behaviour involves fundamentally the so-called action frame of reference but, in order to investigate the varying degrees to which the effects of the various laws intertwine, Pareto was forced into the construction of a mechanical model of society based upon a crude classification of human motives, in which the circulation of élites proceeded from set 'residues' present within the human psyche. The system was constructed so that artificial interferences with it would cause changes within the system leading to a modification of its normal state. The vagueness of this notion of equilibrium, the positivistic rigidity of Pareto's classification and the political value judgments which underlie much of his writing combine to give an aura of ideology and pseudoscience to his work. This impression is, in my estimation, justified for although much of his influence has been acknowledged by other 'systems theorists' who still speak of 'world wars powerfully suggesting the permeability of system boundaries', Pareto is perhaps more acknowledged as one of the sociologists who first gave detailed treatment to the problem of the emergence of élite groups and the maintenance of their power. By and large, the 'systematic' elements within his theory have been relegated, and rightly so, to the status of intellectual curiosities.

Although the concept of mechanical equilibrium is now dead as a sociological model, a modifiable form of interdependence theory designed to meet the familiar Paretian problem of the variety of 'intertwining causes' and effects is very much alive. The formulation of this theory owes as much to the traditional organic analogies of political and social philosophy as to Pareto. The concept of equilibrium, however, occupies a key place in interdependence theories especially in its particular manifestation as homeostasis. One can readily understand how attractive homeostatic models of society may appear to the sociologist, distressed both by the complexity of social 'variables' and his own lack of an adequate empirical methodology through which to isolate them and investigate their interrelations.

The organicist analogy—of society as living organism, fighting to maintain its survival and integrity dependent upon the 'normality' of its functioning and upon the 'harmonious' operation of its individual 'members' within a coherent and stable whole—contains within it the seeds of enough relatively diverse political philosophies to dignify it by the application of the word 'holistic'. The emergence of 'holist' and 'atomistic' schools of political and social thought has served only to darken the already twilight landscapes of political philosophy. I haven't the space to explore the ramifications of this particular debate. I want rather to restrict my discussion more closely to the application of the concept of 'homeostasis' with its associated notions of boundary maintenance and negative and positive feedback, within 'the social system', as constructed by the single most influential functionalist sociologist, Talcott Parsons.

Parsons's work has, of course, been subject to the most searching criticism and violent attack on a variety of grounds. Claims have been made that his system is non-explanatory, empty of empirical content, logically incoherent and ideologically biased.[10] I shall be concerned with all these criticisms in so far as they affect Parsons's main thesis that the concept of 'function' can be most usefully applied in sociology by relating the term to the notion of an articulated social system.

Parsons, as has often been remarked, is centrally concerned with the problem of the emergence and maintenance of the social order. All societies exhibit a general tendency, argues Parsons, to maintain themselves as relatively ordered entities since there exists a natural (Hobbesian) tendency towards the atomisation, fragmentation and isolation of these individuals who compose a social 'whole' in the absence of various kinds of social constraints, which arise from the process of interaction. Order, Parsons argues, is maintained generally either by the imposition of coercive restraints upon individuals by more powerful individuals or groups, or more typically by a system of rules governing human behaviour which are in some sense voluntarily accepted. 'Acceptance' or recognition of norms of conduct either induced by coercion or by reciprocal acceptance enable men to predict the behaviour of others and organise their lives on the basis of such predictions. It is in virtue of the existence of such behavioural norms that an investigation of patterned behaviour is possible. Societies are viewed as complex structures which are the product of both contemporary patterns of interaction and interactions from the past which have survived in the form of social institutions. Sociological analysis is the investigation and explanation of patterned and repetitive items of behaviour within this general framework.

For Parsons, however, the primary and fundamental problem in sociological analysis is not the investigation of specific patterns of behaviour but the setting up of a 'logically articulate conceptual scheme'—a logically interrelated set of categories or concepts—which exhausts the logical possibilities of interaction and provides a conceptual scheme in which the posing of the question 'How is social order possible?' can be most fruitfully set. In providing such a scheme, Parsons has to face the crucial problem of including within a conceptual scheme elements which allow a 'voluntaristic' dimension to human behaviour whilst at the same time incorporating the concept of a social system which is relatively deterministic. Given an *a priori* commitment to voluntarism, Parsons has to locate the deterministic element in human behaviour as a characteristic of society rather than the individual.[11] It is because the existence of 'society' involves the postulation of certain limits on human behaviour, that the action of the individual is constrained. The answer to the question 'How is society possible?' involves reference to a set of functional prerequisites which must be satisfied in order for a social system to emerge and maintain its existence. Thus individual action is set in a framework of necessary constraints which are dictated by the nature of society in general. Whether Parsons's inquiry into the nature of society is a conceptual or empirical matter does not emerge from his voluminous writings on the question. The so-called functional imperatives seem to be (a) necessary to the definition of a society and (b) an empirically identifiable process within all known societies. Possibly it is Parsons's intention to derive (a) from (b). However that may be, all societies for Parsons are systems in dynamic equilibrium—maintained in any given state of equilibrium not so much by a 'mechanical' balance of conflicting forces as by a system of negative feedback which ensures that, whilst the system is in existence, certain defined processes must occur.

The total context of human behaviour is defined for Parsons by the interaction of three systems[12]—the cultural system, the social system, and the personality system—all based upon the physiological organism. The personality system is primarily the province of the psychologist, who is essentially concerned with 'personality types' or 'individual differences' and their effect upon society. The cultural aspect of action systems is somewhat nebulously supposed to consist of such 'modes of motivational orientation as cognitive, cathectic and evaluative . . . and of . . . systems of ideas or beliefs, systems of expressive symbols and systems of value orientation.'[13] What Parsons has in mind here is presumably those linguistic, ethical, scientific and religious values and ideas which serve as a generalised background influence upon more specific forms of social behaviour. In what sense such vague, general influences constitute a system is not discussed.

A social system is comprised of patterns of behaviour which occur whenever two or more actors are interacting with any other on the basis of a minimal degree of complementary expectation by means of, or according to, a shared system of beliefs, standards and means of communication.

Each of these systems is conceptually autonomous according to Parsons, though empirically they are indissoluble.[14] There appears

also to be a (partially?) deterministic hierarchy within this classification, in which more complex systems 'control' the simpler systems
such as those of the organism or the personality. The link between
the personality and social system is held to reside in the concept of
the 'individual in role'.

Parsons's notion then is of a society as a self-maintaining system
definable in terms of certain functional prerequisites and certain
boundaries which mark it off from other systems or its 'environment'. The conceptual unit of the social system is the role—role
being defined as a sector of the individual actor's total system of
action. The emphasis is upon stability, upon the normative *order*
within the system. Such an order is not regarded as total, however,
for a society in equilibrium can tolerate certain internal strains. It
is when the strains become in some sense 'crucial' that the system
moves to a new state of equilibrium. Furthermore, changes in the
'external environment' can lead to a change in the state of
equilibrium.

The conceptual basis of Parsons's thought is not only complex
and slippery but it is difficult to isolate any particular concept for
analysis without facing the criticism that one is neglecting the
analysis of the system as a whole. Edward Devereux, one of Parsons's
most lucid expositers, for example, writes of Parsons's 'exasperating
tendency to insist that each and every point in his entire system
is fundamental'. Nevertheless, one has to attach meaning to Parsons's
concepts in order to begin to see their interrelationship and having
sketched in the elements of Parsonian theory I now intend to examine
more closely his usage of the word 'equilibrium'.

Parsons implicitly or explicitly uses the word equilibrium in a
variety of ways. They may be summarised as follows:

(a) *Equilibrium (1)* The assertion that all 'variables' within a social
    system are *interdependent*, changes in the 'value of one entailing
    changes in the value of others' (except where the system tolerates
    'strain').
(b) *Equilibrium (2)* Here the analogy is with the homeostatic
    model used in the biological sciences.
(c) *Equilibrium (3)* The explicit conditions for maintenance of
    equilibrium are based upon an analogy with the ideal laws of
    Newtonian mechanics.

(d) *Equilibrium (4)* Equilibrium is here defined as the persistence
  of stable reciprocities between interacting actors.

These usages are not logically distinct as elaborated here and
neither are they in Parsons's work. Rather the concept of equilibrium
has for Parsons a range of application and an intermeshing of logical
categories. Any one use of the word equilibrium carries with it
overtones and images of other usages. Thus the homeostatic model,
probably the central one, is larded over with the associations of
equilibrium as mutual dependence and persistence of stable reciprocities. This fact makes full understanding of the concept virtually
impossible, short of a detailed retranslation of Parsons's entire
terminology.

Parsons, however, appears to regard the concept of equilibrium
as vital to the practice of social science. He writes, for example:[15]

Equilibrium, in short, is nothing but the concept of regularity
under specific conditions as applied to the internal state of an
empirical system relative to its environment. This regularity of
course should always be treated as relative rather than absolute;
indeed, it is generally subject to considerable ranges of tolerance,
and of course its maintenance is by no means inevitable but, if the
conditions on which it depends are changed beyond certain limits,
it will disappear, again most probably giving way to other
regularities than to sheer randomness. Thus in my opinion this
concept is an inherently essential part of the logic of science, of
importance proportionate to the level of theoretical generality
aimed at. The denial of its legitimacy in the conceptual armoury
of social science is at least, in my perhaps not very humble
opinion symptomatic of the denial that social science itself is
legitimate, or realistically possible. On this point I have thus
remained completely unimpressed by the barrage of persistent
criticism.

This usage seems to be basically that referred to as equilibrium (1)
but Parsons illustrates this abstract statement by reference to
'Cannon's famous concept of homeostasis'. He refers to the human
organism's ability to maintain a constant body temperature as a
'special case of equilibrium'.

In the 'Working Papers',[16] however, he lists the generalised conditions of equilibrium as follows :

1 *The Principle of Inertia:* A given process of action will continue unchanged in rate and direction unless impeded or deflected by opposing motivational force.

2 *The Principle of Action and Reaction:* If, in a system of action, there is a change in the direction of a process, it will tend to be balanced by a complementary change which is equal in motivational force and opposite in direction.

3 *The Principle of Effort:* Any change in the rate of an action process is directly proportional to the magnitude of the motivational force applied or withdrawn.

4 *The Principle of System-Maintenance:* Any pattern element (mode of organisation of components) within a system of action will tend to be confirmed in its place within the system or to be eliminated from the system (extinguished) as a function of its contribution to the integrative balance of the system (Working Paper 102–3).

Such phrases as 'directly proportional to the magnitude of the motivational force applied or withdrawn' strike me, frankly, as unintelligible pseudoscience. Whilst many of the Parsonian concepts such as the pattern variables do act as (dubious) classificatory schemes enabling one to categorise like social processes at a micro-level, the attempt to establish 'idealised laws' governing the non-mathematical relationships between social process and psychological 'forces' seems an exercise in empty verbalism.

There is also a further tendency to equate the notion of equilibrium with the notion of 'harmony' in social relationships. There is evidence of this tendency in Parsons, in virtue of this use of the equilibrium (4)—that involving the notion of stable patterns of reciprocal interaction.[17]

We may assume that if alter's motivational pattern is fully integrated with the norm and has sufficient 'resiliency' not to be thrown out of equilibrium, by the strain put upon by ego's incipient deviance, the sanctions he will impose will tend to be such as to tend to re-equilibrate ego's action with the norm. There is of course a wide range of variation of the possible specific elements involved, but broadly we may assume first that on the one hand alter will tend to act in such a way as to influence ego's situation in the direction of making it advantageous for ego in reality terms to return to conformity, and second that alter's attitudes will be such as, with ambivalence, to show his disapproval of the direction ego's action is taking.

Here, there is a tendency to equate 'the return to conformity' to a return to a state of equilibrium—though these two concepts seem distinguishable. Indeed the use of equilibrium (3) appears to add weight to the charge of implicit political conservatism in the Parsonian model. Emphasis upon the normative order of society, upon 'a science of social statics' in which social equilibrium is in part identified with conformity to social norms, involves Parsons in the grotesque problems of defining the 'needs of the social system and social goals'. It is significant that whenever Devereux wishes to illustrate Parsons's theory, he uses examples drawn from a military context (e.g. a US Navy destroyer) where the 'goals of the system' are less ambiguous than those of a 'total society'.

But perhaps the most damning criticism of Parsons's concept of equilibrium is its pretentiousness. Robert Brown[18] has noted that in the physical sciences and in economics, the term equilibrium is only employed when 'we know what properties are said to be in equilibrium how they are to be measured, and what conditions are held constant'.

Now clearly these criteria are not satisfied in the social sciences at the 'macro-level' of analysis nor is it possible to interpret such concepts as 'the boundary of a social system' in any precise way. What the notion of 'system' seems to exclude in sociology is a condition of anarchy; what the notion of equilibrium asserts is that existing institutional arrangements often resist change. At this level one may well agree with Max Black that the component concepts of Parsons's scheme are laymen's concepts in the thin disguise of a technical sounding terminology.

(ii) Degenerate theory : Coser's theory of social conflict.

Apart from some critical remarks about the 'intellectual dishonesty' of Marx and Freud, Lakatos does not specify examples of what he calls a 'degenerative problem shift' within the field of the social sciences. There are however, clear examples to be drawn upon from the voluminous 'theoretical' literature. I propose to take only one: Lewis Coser's attempt to meet objections by so-called 'conflict' theorists to functionalist analysis.

Lakatos has a clear statement of a degenerative problem shift. He writes:[19] 'If we put forward a theory to resolve a contradiction between a previous theory and a counter example in such a way that the new theory instead of offering a content increasing (scientific) *explanation* only offers a content decreasing (linguistic) *reinterpretation*, the contradiction is resolved in a merely semantical, unscientific way.' Mere semantical reinterpretations, then, are what distinguish degenerative from progressive problem shifts. Let me now apply this criterion to Coser's work as exemplified in *The Functions of Social Conflict*.[20]

Coser's book is both a commentary upon the work of Georg Simmel and an attempt to meet objections to functionalist forms of explanation. Coser uses Simmel's insights to strengthen functionalist theory by treating 'conflict' as a mechanism whereby social cohesion is maintained. Parsons's treatment of conflict and deviance in terms of 'strains' and 'tensions' within a system maintained in a state of equilibrium Coser finds unsatisfactory, but he also holds that 'commitment to the view that social conflict is necessarily destructive of the relationship within which it occurs leads . . . to highly deficient interpretations.'[21]

Crudely, then, Coser is working towards a resolution of two 'theoretical' approaches towards sociological analysis, one of which stresses the significance of the 'Hobbesian problem of order' and sees its resolution in terms of such concepts as 'normative *consensus*' and another, diametrically opposed approach, where conflict of interest and power relationships are crucial to the understanding of the social structure and the social processes which occur within it. For consensus theorists, social conflict is an anomaly standing in need of special explanation; for conflict theorists social cohesion is to be understood primarily in terms of the coercion of so-called subordinate groups rather than in terms of 'consent'—explicit or implied. Now clearly social order is maintained both by agreement upon the rules whereby people conduct their lives and by sanctions which support such rules or exact penalties from those who deviate

from them. The point at issue between the two 'schools' is whether
and to what extent agreement upon certain 'functional prerequisites'
is a necessary condition for the maintenance and persistence of social
order. The Hobbesian problem of how men ever come together in
social groups is resolved by consensus theorists in terms of some such
concept as the 'internalisation of rules' and by the conflict theorists
in terms of the coercion of the weak. The argument is thus about the
importance to be attached to consensus and conflict in the explanation of social behaviour.

Both 'theoretical' approaches need to demonstrate the *subsidiary
role* played by either conflict or consensus respectively in the analysis
of social behaviour. Coser, for example, attempts to demonstrate
that conflict 'far from being a "negative" factor which "tears apart",
. . . may fulfil a number of determinate functions in groups and
other interpersonal relations; it may, for example, contribute to the
maintenance of group boundaries.'

Before analysing Coser's arguments, however, it is necessary to
make some brief comment upon the status of these two theories. In
opposition though they are, they share common attributes as
follows:

(a) The level of generality at which they are asserted makes the
'theories' compatible with both widely similar and widely different
empirical states of affairs. That is to say, unambiguous potential
empirical confirmations or disconfirmations of the theories are difficult to come by.

(b) As a consequence of (a) counter-examples to either 'theory' are
likely to be couched in terms which have either little direct empirical
reference or which are ambiguous in relation to actual states of
affairs.

(c) Neither 'theory' can make unambiguous predictions.

(d) The notion that either conflict or consensus plays a 'subsidiary
role' is not one that can be unambiguously formulated.

There are thus marked differences between these 'theories' and
models of successful theory within the physical sciences. But what
is of interest at present is less the status of these 'theories' than the
response of their advocates to challenge or criticism. For, as I hope
to demonstrate, the essential ambiguity of the theories allows for
the 'digesting of anomalies' only through a process of semantic

reinterpretation rather than through content-increasing explanation.

Coser draws his immediate inspiration from the work of Simmel.[22] Simmel argues that analysis systematically distorts the nature of the real world. The whole social process is, for him, homogeneous, but the ability to portray the homogeneity depends upon distinguishing for the purpose of analysis that which is inherently indistinguishable in life. Thus Simmel writes: 'Definite, actual society does not result only from social forces which are positive and only to the extent that negative forces hinder them.' On the contrary: 'both factors of interaction manifest themselves as wholly positive.'

Conflict, argues Simmel, is clearly a possible candidate as a 'form of sociation'; conflict embodies a positive response (it is to be distinguished, for example, from 'indifference'); conflict relationships do not always counteract unity—conflict in fact integrates. We do not see this clearly because we are bemused by an 'analytic separation' of these elements. Coser seeks to illustrate this apparently paradoxical view by setting out no less than sixteen propositions of Simmel where conflict can be seen as a binding force in social relationships. I want briefly to analyse a number of these propositions in order to show how a series of semantic shifts enables Coser to accommodate the facts of conflict within a functionalist framework.[23]

Proposition 1

A certain amount of discord, inner divergence and outer controversy, is organically tied up with the very elements that ultimately hold the group together . . . the positive and integrating role of antagonism is shown in structures which stand out by the sharpness and carefully preserved purity of their social diversions and graduations. Thus, the Hindu social system rests not only on the hierarchy, but also directly on the mutual repulsion of the castes. Hostilities not only prevent boundaries within the group from gradually disappearing . . . often they provide classes and individuals with reciprocal positions which they would not find . . . if the causes of hostility were not accompanied by the feeling and the expression of hostility.

It is quite clear that conflict *between* groups tends to maintain the boundary lines of the groups and reinforces notions of group identity, but the Simmelian claim goes further than this. The argument is that 'the Hindu social system rests . . . directly on the mutual repulsion of the castes'. What this implies is as follows:

(a) Hostility towards out-groups leads to a reinforcement of in-group solidarity.

(b) Reinforcement of group solidarity renders social mobility unlikely.

Hence

(c) A stratification system of closed castes is directly maintained by hostility.

and

(d) Feelings of mutual hostility are functional for the system.

There are two points to be made here: first, the stability of the caste system is clearly maintained by factors which are not internal to the systems, and second, a distinction between 'feelings of hostility' and 'open conflict' is necessary if the example is to be clearly related to the thesis that conflict is functional for integration.

The Hindu caste system is clearly one where conflicts, defined as direct antagonistic transactions between individuals, are *contained* and *under control*. Any system of stratification is potentially explosive; that is, conflicts and resentments on the part of subordinate groups are always likely to be potentially disruptive. That hostile attitudes or sentiments do not break out into open conflict is a consequence of the operation of both coercive or internalised normative controls—the latter often buttressed by the possibility of the employment of sanctions. Thus what holds the system together is a complex pattern of control procedures built up over time. Hostility between groups within this system may help more sharply to demarcate lines of division, but they in no way help to maintain the *system*. If, for example, I am a self-conscious member of a group B whose position is subordinate in the system to A, I may feel hostile towards A but be dedicated to reversing the respective group positions within the hierarchy. That I may be unable to do so is a product of the fact that controls on the behaviour of the group are exercised *independently* of my feelings of hostility and desire to enter into overt conflict. The system survives *in spite of my hostilities* because 'sociative factors' are operating elsewhere perhaps through an already existing set of *power* relationships. Thus the case that either hostility or conflict is 'functional for integration' is a seriously misleading way of putting a common-sense insight.

Proposition 2

The opposition of a member to an associate is no purely negative social factor, if only because such opposition is often the only means for making life with actually unbearable people at least possible. If we did not even have the power and the right to rebel against tyranny, arbitrariness, moodiness, tactlessness, we could not bear to have any relation to people from whose characters we thus suffer. We would feel pushed to take desperate steps—and these, indeed, would end the relation but do *not*, perhaps, constitute 'conflict'. Not only because of the fact that . . . oppression usually increases if it is suffered calmly and without protest, but also because opposition gives us inner satisfaction, distraction, relief . . . Our opposition makes us feel that we are not completely victims of the circumstances.

Coser comments on this proposition :

Simmel here asserts that the expression of hostility in conflict serves positive functions in so far as it permits the maintenance of relationships under conditions of stress thus preventing group dissolution through the withdrawal of hostile participants : Conflict is thus seen as performing group-maintaining functions in so far as it regulates systems of relationships. It 'clears the air', i.e. it eliminates the accumulation of blocked and baulked hostilities.

Coser cites examples of this so-called 'safety-valve' function of conflict at both the psychological and institutional level. Aggression may be displaced on to other persons or objects leading to tension release; hostile feelings may be expressed and conflict resolved through the operation of socially sanctioned procedures, e.g. through the institution of duelling or through competitive sport. Thus for Coser conflict binds people together in the sense that the avoidance of conflict might lead to withdrawal from a set of social relationships.

Disruption is reduced, he argues, by the displacement of hostile sentiments.

Now it is clearly true that the expression of hostility in open conflict may release tension or avoid the necessity to withdraw from a hostile situation. But in such cases the problem is surely that conflict and hostility is viewed as potentially disruptive. The question is one of how to handle this with the *minimum* degree of actual disruption of relationships which are sought to be maintained for other reasons.

Clearly if I value a relationship which nevertheless generates hostilities it is open to me either to direct my hostility on to other less valued people or objects; or to engage in ritual aggression with the person concerned; or I may withdraw from the situation. What prevents withdrawal, however, is a desire to maintain benefits from the relationship into which I have entered. It would clearly be more advantageous if I could continue to receive such benefits *without* the possibility of conflicts arising, but given that they will arise, I need a technique for *diminishing* their disruptive influences. Thus it is not the existence of conflict or hostility that binds me to another, it is a combination of the fact that I *value* the relationship taken together with an ability to divert potential sources of disruption into non-damaging areas.

Simmel seems both to acknowledge this point and to mystify it:

Proposition 5

While antagonism by itself does not produce sociation, it is a sociological element almost never absent in it . . . This probably is often the situation in respect to the so-called mixture of converging and diverging currents within a group. That is, the structure may be *sui generis* . . . and only in order to be able to describe and understand it, do we put it together, *post factum*, out of two tendencies, one monistic, the other antagonistic. Erotic relations offer the most frequent illustrations. How often do they not strike us as woven together of love and respect, or disrespect . . . But what the observer or the participant himself divides into two intermingling trends may in reality be only one.

Coser illustrates and expands Simmel's point by noting Malinowski's dictum that 'aggression is a by-product of co-operation' and by comparing Simmel's views to the Freudian notion of ambivalence. In what Simmel refers to as intimate 'dyadic' relationships, hostilities are seen as potentially more damaging than in contractual relationships, yet they appear to be a necessary feature of close relationships. This gives weight, it may be thought, to Simmel's notion that each interactive situation is *sui generis*—one in which elements of sociation and conflict are bound together. But as Coser himself notes, Simmel's mystical approach fails to bring out a crucial distinction between conflicts which arise '*within* the same consensual framework' and conflicts which 'put the basic consensus in question'.

Where conflicts or hostility may *not* prove to be disruptive is in situations where (a) there are *agreed procedures* for conflict resolution and (b) where conflict does not impinge upon those shared values which are the *basis* of the co-operation.

This distinction illustrates the fact that, providing there is agreement upon 'basic issues' democratic or pluralist societies can tolerate a high degree of open conflict. And certainly Coser is right when he asserts conflict in such situations is not necessarily an 'index of low stability'. But Coser's thesis is *not* simply that the existence of open conflict or hostility is not always to be taken to be a good indicator of instability. He holds that, in a significant sense, conflict is *functional* for societal and psychological co-operation and integration.

Thus in relation to the 'conflict-consensus' debate what Coser has done is to take cases where the existence of conflict and hostility are *compatible* with a high degree of integration and treat them as if they were *causally operative in establishing and maintaining consensus*. That is, he has resolved an anomaly in his theoretical position by a linguistic re-interpretation of 'conflict' so as to fit a prior theoretical model. No doubt his commentary on Simmel's propositions contain illuminating insights into the way in which conflict, hostility and consensus are related in typical empirical situations. What he has not shown is that conflict and hostility can be regarded as anything more nor less than potentially or actually disruptive in social relationships. In terms of the '*theoretical*' debate, any theoretical extension or empirical research programme based upon this invalid re-interpretation is certain to prove to be increasingly degenerate.

(iii) Propositional sociology : empirical generalisations and causal
    linkages

'Discovery', writes George C. Homans[24] 'is the job of stating and
testing more or less general relationships between properties of
nature'. Theories for Homans are expressed in propositional form.
'Real theory', he writes, 'consists precisely of propositions'. Concepts
such as 'role' and 'culture' are useful only as non-operating definitions. Parsonian 'theory' is the multiplication of non-operating
definitions into a non-operating conceptual scheme. 'Real' propositions
are not to be confused with such 'orienting statements'—they are
empirical generalisations of a high order. Theory is like a game:
'The winner is the man who can deduce the largest variety of
empirical findings from the smallest number of general propositions.'
    Homans accepts in its entirety one special view of the nature of
explanation. Explanation of human behaviour is only possible by
subsuming what is to be explained under a covering law. All explanation, in ordinary discourse, history, sociology or physics must,
it appears, be tested against this model. The collation of general
propositions which assert regularities within human conduct in
diverse particular situations is seen as distinctively sociological.
Further, much sociological theory has been merely 'orienting' or
'methodological' according to Homans. The equilibrium model merely
asserts, for example, that given a change in x there will be a corresponding change in y. Homans comments dramatically : 'Don't
just tell me there will be some change. Tell me *what* change. Stand
and Deliver !'
    The deficiencies of much that passes under the name of sociological
theory makes easy the acceptance of the covering law view of explanation for empirically minded sociologists. If one is interested in
tightening up and evaluating sociological explanations, then the
covering law model offers immediate rewards. It offers a concise
ideal of explanation; it is 'scientifically' respectable; it can be interpreted so as to fall short of the demands of *theoretical* explanation
in the physical sciences and yet still qualify as *the* appropriate form
of explanation; it enables one to incorporate into the methodology
of the social sciences a refusal to admit speculative or non-operating
theories or definitions as being explanatory.
    Hans L. Zetterberg,[25] for example, distinguishes 'Social Theory'

which, he argues, is humanistic and value-loaded from 'Sociological Theory' which is constituted by 'multivariate empirical generalisations'. Social Theory, a category which includes most 'classic' works in sociology, provides clues, indicates directions of study and fills in the detailed content of implicit sociological laws. Sociological Theory, on the other hand, packs into a set of propositions information which is applicable to a wide range of empirical situations.

Both Zetterberg and Homans seem enamoured of Berelson and Steiner's *Human Behavior: an inventory of findings*[26] in which there occur 1,045 numbered propositions of varying degrees of generality which, taken together and subsumed under more highly general laws, presumably constitute sociological theory. These one thousand odd propositions include the following:

(a) Prolonged unemployment typically leads to a deterioration of personality, passivity, apathy, anomie, listlessness, dissociation, lack of interest and caring.
(b) A person's self-evaluation is strongly influenced by the ranking of his 'class' by society.
(c) TV viewing by children is heaviest amongst the duller and emotionally insecure.
(d) The more people associate with one another under conditions of equality, the more they come to share values and norms, the more they come to like one another.
(e) People prejudiced against one ethnic group tend to be prejudiced against others.

These propositions, according to Zetterberg, become a 'theory' when they are interrelated; they are 'explained' when they are subsumed under other empirical generalisations; they are 'verified' when from the combination of empirical generalisations, new generalisations are deduced and tested empirically.

If the results of empirical analysis are to be expressed in propositional form, then, suggests Zetterberg, three questions need to be answered:

(a) What are the *determinants* and results actually entering the proposition?
(b) What linkages are presumed between the 'variables' within a proposition?
(c) What is the *informative value* of the proposition?

First, propositions must relate at least two 'variates' although in fact two variate propositions in sociology are held by Zetterberg to be 'generally suspect'. Consider for example Homans's proposition: 'If the frequency of interaction between two or more persons increases, the degree of liking of one another will increase and vice versa.'

Such a proposition was useful as a beginning, argues Zetterberg: it asserts a definite testable (but false!) generalisation. Additional variates, however, need to be incorporated into the proposition to safeguard it from falsity. He prefers Malewski's[27] new formulation: 'If the costs of avoiding interaction are too low and if there are available alternative sources of reward, the more frequent the interaction, the greater the mutual liking.'

This proposition refers to the social psychology of individuals within a dyadic or group situation. If it is true and if it avoids tautology it does indicate a certain regularity of behaviour exhibited by people in interaction.

The essential ambiguity of the proposition, however, rests upon its use of so-called 'exchange theory' which works on the simple psychological basis that man, when acting, seeks to minimise his costs and maximise his rewards. The 'theory' when operating with a quantified monetary definition of cost and reward might prove useful to economists in combination with other general postulates about the behaviour of 'economic man' in a market economy but it carries with it little positive information in a psychological sense. Indeed such a proposition virtually reduces to the tautology that a 'man will act as he will act' unless we assume that certain things may be regarded as 'costs' and 'rewards' across the board of human cultures. One man's cost, however, is frequently another man's reward, when what is to count as 'cost and reward' begin to be specified.

In Malewski's proposition, the clauses 'if there are available alternative sources of reward' and 'if the costs of avoiding interaction are low' are introduced to set qualifications of the very highest level of generality upon Homans's previously enunciated proposition linking 'liking' and 'interaction'. What can be deduced from this proposition is not likely to be of high informative value given the wide range of reference of the qualifications implicit in the terms 'cost' and 'reward'. Thus, in answering the question 'What are the determinants and results entering the proposition?' Zetterberg exposes the central weaknesses of sociological propositions—their openness to *ceteris paribus* qualification. Indeed, of the propositions (a) to (e) cited in Berelson and Steiner, one might comment that each one is either empty, trivial, or empirically dubious without further qualifications; certainly each 'finding' either coheres with or repeats our ordinary assumptions about human psychology or it stands in need of further qualification, confirmation and explanation.

All linkages between propositions are for Zetterberg, causal. He acknowledges, however, that there may be 'varieties' of causal linkages. Having identified precisely the determinants which occur in 'multivariate propositions' the sociologist then has to specify and assess the nature of the causal linkage. Zetterberg lists five types of causal linkage as follows:

(1)   (a) *Reversible*   (b) *Irreversible*

These linkages take the form:

(a) if X then Y; if Y then X.

an example being Homans's proposition linking frequency of interaction with mutual liking:

(b) if X then Y; if Y—no conclusion about X.

The distinction here is presumably between a straightforward hypothetical proposition (1b) and one which is strengthened such that one can by affirming the consequent guarantee the antecedent.

(2)   (a) *Deterministic*   (b) *Stochastic*

These take the form:

(a) If X then Y.
(b) If X then probably (generally interpreted in a statistical sense) Y.

Zetterberg notes that (2a) is 'very rare in sociology' and (2b) 'very common'. He cites as an example of (2b): 'A person conforms to a norm rather than abandons high rank'.

(3)   (a) *Sequential*   (b) *Co-extensive*

This is a very curious distinction of the form:

(a) If X then later Y.
(b) If X then also Y.

E

Examples given are as follows:

(a) If voters are subjected to cross-pressures they are liable to delay their voting decision;
(b) The higher the rate of social mobility, the less the acceptance by the lower classes of militant class ideology.

The distinction is presumably introduced (1a) to allow for the possibility for a causal time-lag. Stress is placed on the antecedent nature of the causal influence. The example, however, is ambiguous. Do the cross-pressures cause a *delay* in coming to a decision or do they influence voting decisions taken at a later time? Presumably both—as in both cases cross-pressures are temporarily prior to an action or to its inhibition.

In (b), writes Zetterberg, 'no assumption is made that mobility occurred before or after the spread of working class ideology'. The 'causal' categorisation marks mere concomitance. Nevertheless, the formulation of the example strongly indicates a temporal relationship, i.e., the rate of social mobility is taken to be a causal influence on the acceptance or otherwise of militant class ideology. The proposition does not seem to be reversible. Perhaps (2b) ought to be reformulated as follows: Changes in X are accompanied by changes in Y—the causal relationship being left open.

(4) (a) *Sufficient*   (b) *Contingent*

These take the form:

(a) If X then Y regardless of anything else.
(b) If X then Y but only if Z.

Here (4a) seems to be a reiteration of the Deterministic category whilst (4b) seems to hint at the possibility of so-called multiple causation.

(5) (a) *Necessary*   (b) *Substitutable*

These take the form:

(a) If X and only if X then Y.
(b) If X then Y but also if Z then Y.

In (5b) the quasi-causal use of the term 'function' is implicit (i.e., when effect Y is observed, X is assumed [or Z or any other plausible 'functional equivalents']).

In illustrating the use of these distinctions, Zetterberg categorises Weber's proposition connecting the Protestant Ethic with the emergence of the spirit of capitalism as 'irreversible, stochastic, sequential, contingent and substitutable'. That is, Weber's thesis exhibits very weak forms of causal linkages and thus from a propositionalist point of view[28] it is rather unsatisfactory since implicit in Zetterberg's analysis is the assumption that 'causally-soft' accounts of social phenomena are not 'really' or 'fully' explanatory—that is, they fall short of the covering-law ideal.

Combined with the categories of interdependence and function (which Zetterberg treats separately although they are implicit in his fivefold analysis) these causal categories are distinguished in order that *deductions* of lower-order propositions from more general propositions are given proper weight. In any deductive system linking propositions, the causal linkage between determinants must be of the 'same type'.

Distinctively theoretical propositions are thus those in which the determinants, results and causal linkages may be precisely defined and in which the 'informative value' of the proposition is clear. In general, claims Zetterberg, 'the larger the number of ways a proposition can be proved, incorrect, the higher its informative value'. 'Theory' collects low-value information (ordinary) propositions and subsumes them under high-value (theoretical) informative propositions.

The important consequence of the expression of sociological propositions in axiomatic form and the subsumption of lower-order propositions under more general propositions is that it leads to the emergence of *new* propositions which can be tested empirically—thus building up an interconnected tissue of substantive theory. On a recombination of axioms, suitable expressed, argues Zetterberg, new propositions appear.

Assume that the following propositions are given, suggests Zetterberg:

(1) If national prosperity increases, then the middle classes expand.

(2) If the middle classes expand, then the consensus of values in the society increases.

(3) If the middle classes expand, then social mobility increases.

(4) If social mobility increases the consensus of values increases and vice versa.

Proposition (3) is in fact deducible from the combination of propositions (2) and (4) (given the important reversibility qualification in (4)) but further, it can be deduced both that :

(5) If national prosperity increases then the consensus of values increases;

and,

(6) If national prosperity increases then social mobility increases.

Propositions (5) and (6) are 'new knowledge' in the sense that they were implicit but unrecognised in existing verified propositions.

Now this neat little exercise in elementary traditional logic certainly does expose in a formal way the implications of existing empirical generalisations. The question is, however, whether the existing propositions are sufficiently precise to give the exercise anything but a kind of spurious formal validity. The problem is not about the axiomatic method as such, but about the nature of what is claimed in the 'given'.

In Zetterberg's terms the propositions (1)–(4) are 'stochastic'— merely probable. But their *degree* of probability in British or American society and more importantly in other cultures is exceptionally difficult to assess. Furthermore, to operationalise the term 'value-consensus' in propositions (2) and (4) presents the sociologist with overwhelming problems as does the formulation of unambiguous indicators of 'national prosperity'.

Furthermore, the explanatory force of these propositions is in question. Allowing that the propositions (1)–(6) are 'general facts' of a high degree of probability, they remain statements of fact nevertheless. The 'theoretical' (speculative) explanation of these general facts remains a further question. Of course it is perfectly permissible to argue that the word 'theory' ought to be confined to the activity of collating and exhibiting the various complex relationships between high order empirical generalisations. But the crunch comes when one tries, not merely to uncover 'new' propositions by a re-arrangement of terms, but when one tries to deduce new particular facts from the existing generalisations. In fact most sociological propositions hedged in as they are with *ceteris paribus* qualifications are not amenable to strict treatment upon the lines of some ideal hypothetico-deductive method; nor do they rule out a sufficient number of empirical states of affairs as possible.

Let us consider two apparently diametrically opposed propositions: (although in fact both might be true or both false).

(a) Political apathy is 'eufunctional' (necessary and desirable?) for democracy (since it inhibits the emergence of extremist groups).
(b) Political apathy is 'dysfunctional' for democracy (since the democratic process presupposes a high level of participation in voluntary associations of all kinds).

Now clearly this controversy would gain by being formulated in axiomatic terms. The process of analysis might very well reveal confusions, ambiguities and errors in the expression of the respective 'theories' which were used to formulate and support the propositions. But no universal set of propositions expressed in axiomatic form could hope adequately to express the full import of this particular debate because the complex *ceteris paribus* qualifications and the historical contingencies involved in the application of these propositions preclude their being treated as axioms in a system of law-like propositions. Rather they mark off sets of, in this case, contrary expectations, with which the sociologist or historian comes to an analysis of contingent human behaviour.

This is not to deny however that the 'axiomatic method' is not a useful procedure for sociologists to adopt in *clarifying* their thinking. Clearly such a method does highlight the 'causally-soft' nature of much traditional theorising. Propositionalists, however, aim at more than clarification, they aim to gain acceptance of a new paradigm of theoretical explanation. Ironically their endeavours only reveal both the enormous contingent difficulties of handling the causal relationships between 'variables' in the social situation and the emptiness of the high-level propositions which they regard as potentially the best candidate for theoretical status. Perhaps then a resolution of the 'causal problem' might be achieved by abandoning the strict empiricist concept of theory in favour of 'causally-soft' accounts which nevertheless incorporate that degree of generality which might serve to distinguish sociological explanations from those given by historians.

(iv) Quasi-causal historical theories

Earlier it was suggested that the apparent 'unanswerability' of the Weberian problem[29] raised questions about the appropriateness of the questions raised in discussing the relationship between so-called macrovariables. But the Weberian hypothesis relating religious and economic 'variables' cannot be lightly dismissed. It is regarded by many historically sensitive sociologists of some reputation as being a model of sociological inquiry. Indeed, sociologically sympathetic historians like E. H. Carr though rejecting any notion that Weber had demonstrated a law-like relationship between the spirit of capitalism and the Protestant ethic nevertheless are prepared to regard the Weberian thesis as 'a hypothesis modified *to some extent* in the course of the enquiries which it inspired'.[30]

Now clearly Weber in writing the Protestant ethic, was not concerned merely to give an historical account, couched in narrative terms, of the rise of capitalism. His treatment of the issues is distinct from that generally undertaken by historians yet his analysis of the relationship between the Protestant ethic and the spirit of capitalism was a self-conscious attempt to spell out more precisely the assumptions made by historians through their use of general and abstract concepts. Historians cannot write history without a process of winnowing, selection and the use of concepts which are not empirically primitive. What Weber sought to do was to give the notion of such abstract concepts some clearly defined meaning in terms of which historical analysis could become more self-conscious and more amenable to exact formulation.

In consideration of the Weberian thesis there are three central issues to be analysed : first, there is the strength and consistency of the argument itself; second, there is the question of the degree of empirical support for the thesis; and third, there is his use of the concept of the ideal type—its historical validity and logical structure. Though separable for the purposes of analysis, the three issues are throughout Weber's writings interconnected. Thus, the consistency of Weber's argument is necessarily linked with the general validity of ideal-typification and the evaluation of the logic of the ideal-type depends upon its relationship to contingent historical fact.

Weber's thesis was that Calvinistic Protestantism was a causal determinant in the development of a specific set of mental attitudes towards capitalist economic activity and hence a determinant of that activity in itself. Central to this thesis was a quite specific definition of capitalism as a 'continuously, rationally conducted enterprise' oriented to the 'attainment of profit within a system of market relationships'. Such a definition excluded mere 'capitalistic adventures' and based the notion of capitalism upon a set of economic goals pursued in a highly disciplined way within a complex bureaucratic structure which involved 'a certain impersonal devotion' to the tasks of office. Thus Weber's ideal typical capitalist is not, as Professor Leff[31] notes, 'the compound of reason, feeling, principle, self-interest, habit and so on, which animates most men but a rationally calculating entrepreneur dedicated to profit as a calling'.

Now it is interesting to note that not only is Weber's definition of capitalism an abstraction allegedly drawn from the one-sided accentuation of historical reality,[32] but it also builds into the very idea of capitalism the notion of 'a calling'—a specific element in *Calvinistic theology*. Calvin's notion that 'the blessings we enjoy are divine deposits to be dispensed for the benefit of our neighbours' involved the view that social position was a type of stewardship— a hallowed vocation, the 'post-assigned' to be faithfully exercised in the absence of indicators of salvational status. Weber, *within his very definition* of capitalism, draws a parrallel between the structure of Calvinism and bureaucratic capitalism thus persuasively suggesting a connexion between the two prior to any process of argumentation. It is important to recognise this incorporation of what is, after all, merely an analogy into the definition of capitalism since even if the analogy can be shown to be fruitful and suggestive of possible causal connexions it tends to operate as a definitional axiom in the form in which it is presented.

Weber sought to demonstrate a congruence at the level of meaning between the set of mental attitudes characteristic of the ideal typical capitalist and the ethics of the ascetic branches of the Protestant also defined in ideal typical terms. Congruence, or at least compatibility between these two 'systems' of values, would tend to suggest the possibility of causal connexion especially if one could demonstrate a lack of congruence or incompatibility between Catholic and Lutheran values and the spirit of capitalism.

In order to show congruence or compatibility, Weber had to show the following:

(a) Congruence between the ethical and ascetic components in both ideal typical capitalism and the expressed and explicit views of Calvin and his disciples; or

(b) Congruence between the ethical and ascetic components in ideal typical capitalism and the unintended psychological consequences of the acceptance of Calvinistic theology by ordinary men.

The danger here of course is that if (a) is not established, (b) may be speculatively introduced to save the original hypothesis. Weber was not unaware of this danger and tried to show that although Calvin's expressed doctrine was not amenable to such interpretation, later shifts and accommodation in Calvinist theology taken together with the response of ordinary men to the psychological pressures induced by Calvinism could in fact sustain the congruence thesis. Indeed Parsons argues that if one can demonstrate that vulgarised Calvinism and ideal typical capitalism had certain features in common, in view of the complex nature of both systems, 'a close functional relationship becomes highly probable'.

This statement, however, seems to claim far too much. Any system of values, especially systems *constructed* upon the basis of ideal-typification, will on a chance basis tend to have a number of (sometimes key) postulates or attitudes in common. Asceticism for example is widespread in many different religious systems and many different societies. One cannot, on the basis of general similarity of 'value-orientation' in a number of respects infer the likelihood of causal connexions or functional relationships between the systems as such. Such a functional or quasi-causal hypothesis demands close congruence in a number of key respects—in Weber's case an inter-related combination of ascetism and activism needs to be demonstrated together with a wealth of further evidence showing a mutual compatibility in a number of other respects (Calvinist and Zwinglian negative attitudes towards usury and the acquisition of wealth as an end in itself for example need *special* explanation in Weber's thesis).

Calvin's writings were dialectical in nature, full as McNeill notes, of 'unresolved paradoxes and logical tensions'.[33] Central to his theology, however, was an explicit doctrine of 'Double Predestination'. Calvin wrote:[34]

Predestination we call the eternal decree of God by which he has determined with himself what He would have to become of every man. For . . . eternal life is fore-ordained for some and eternal damnation for others. Every man therefore being formed for one or the other of these ends we may say that he is predestinated to life or death.

The elect thus owe to God ceaseless gratitude and obedience whilst the reprobate may not question the wisdom of the dread decree (*decretum horribile*) by which they are left in a state of alienation from God, for as Paul had written (Romans 9 : 18), 'God hath mercy on whom he will have mercy and whom he will be hardeneth'.

Now clearly such a doctrine seems to have political and moral implications which are essentially quietist. For Calvin, God's acts do not admit of moral understanding although 'he who makes God capricious despoils him'. The die for humanity is already cast; the activity broadly recommended is to have faith from which good works will flow and to carry out one's 'vocation' which is the 'post-assigned' by God. Radical action on this earth whether political, moral or economic is beside the point.

It is a feature of many religious systems, however, that their quietist implications can have *both* conservative and radical consequences. It is Weber's contention that the *unintended consequences* of Calvin's doctrine of double predestination were significant in considering the role of religious ideas in relation to economic development. As McNeill notes :

A man's historical influence often appears ironically at variance with its own conscious aims. Calvin's insistence on diligence and frugality, his horror of waste of time or of goods, his permitting interest on money under strict limitations of equity and charity and his similarly grounded permission of change of one's vocation are justly held to have contributed something to the development of capitalist industry and business. Max Weber has convinced many that Calvin's doctrine of election led to a sense of 'unprecedented' inner loneliness and that . . . in *later* Calvinists this induced the quest for vocational success in order to allay anxiety regarding the divine favour, but it should not be overlooked that, for Calvin, this is the basis of an industrious altruism never of unsocial economic individualism.

Thus for Weber it was the unintended consequences of the hard doctrine of double predestination which was significant for the development of the spirit of capitalism. The origins of capitalism being problematic for Weber, one set of 'variables' which were associated with its development qualified for possible causal (though emphatically not mono-causal) status. This set of variables was the influence of ascetic protestantism upon the practical attitudes that large masses of men took towards their everyday activities. Calvinism implied that no wordly indicators of salvation were available; men found this too hard a psychological burden to bear. Thus indicators of salvation were to be located in worldly success coupled with an ascetic life-style. By a selective consideration of later vulgarised Calvinist doctrine Weber attempted to support this speculative hypothesis.

Now it cannot be said that there is nothing of value in Weber's analysis. Far from it. As an exercise in speculative historical intelligence it is subject to just the same intersubjective professional criteria that other historical accounts of the periods must submit. Thus, it has been argued that Weber overstressed the autonomy of religious beliefs, that he misconstrued the relations between religion and economic developments in that religion only operates so as to set certain limits upon the development of economic institutions. However that may be, we are considering the Weberian thesis not as an exercise in speculative historical analysis but as in some sense distinctively sociological—and it is precisely in that sense that Weber fails to satisfy his critics.

If one is seeking to establish a *general* causal thesis, however qualified, between systems of ideas and economic changes, then one's thesis must be backed either by a closely detailed historical analysis grounded in the particularities of time and place or one must adapt and select from historical circumstances to support one's thesis. Weber self-consciously trod this latter path in order to provide a quasi-causal theoretical interpretation of an historical development. The trouble is that this approach, though 'distinctively sociological', does violence to history. The ideal typification of the concepts of capitalism and protestantism involves selection from differing time periods; the *quietist* implications of Calvin's explicit theology are not fully considered; the possible tautologous relationship between the definitions of Calvinism and capitalism are not fully explored;

and the whole case rests upon a very insecure speculative base about the reactions of 'ordinary men' to contemporary theological doctrines and influences. Thus whilst Weber's thesis can be viewed as historically interesting speculation, which has become carefully modified or even substantially changed over time, the 'sociological insights' it exhibited are not so much false as fundamentally *irrelevant*. The historian has no need of the sociologist except in so far as the latter can be interpreted as a *historical critic* by pointing up the importance of hitherto neglected historical considerations and thereby stimulating further research. But most sociologists are not content to see their role as that of under-labourer for the historian. More's the pity !

The relation of sociological and historical explanation will be examined in more detail later. Suffice it to say, at this point, that the possibility of a distinctively sociological approach to historical events which does justice to historical particularity has not been demonstrated in Weber's work. It cannot be doubted, of course, that Weber was a man of profound intelligence with a mastery of much historical detail. But even the most erudite and scholarly of men must needs direct themselves to intellectual ambitions which are in principle realisable.

THE FAILURE OF SOCIOLOGICAL THEORY: *a priori* OR CONTINGENT?

The failure of sociological theorists to generate explanations at the so-called 'macro-level' which successfully emulate theories in the physical sciences raises the question of whether causal and general explanations of human behaviour are possible in principle or are merely contingently difficult to formulate. In some ways, however, the distinction between *a priori* and contingent objections to a science of human behaviour cannot easily be maintained. Arguments which point to the complexity of human action, to the difficulties experienced in locating, controlling and giving meaning to social 'variables' may be mere symptoms of a more fundamental difficulty—that of treating human actions as 'events' on a par with events in the natural world. My own position on this complex issue may be stated quite baldly as follows. I do not believe that sufficient reasons have been adduced to show that the explanation of human behaviour demands, *a priori*, a set of explanatory categories different from those employed in giving an account of natural events. Nevertheless, as I hope to indicate in what follows and in what I have already noted about the inadequacy of sociological theory, the fact is that plausible or acceptable explanations of human behaviour are not generally cast in 'law-like' form nor do they employ the notion of 'cause' in an uncontaminated sense. All explanations of human behaviour involve reference either directly or parasitically to the concept of what it is deemed 'rational' for men to engage in.

Now these contingent facts about the nature of the explanation of human behaviour may *strongly suggest* the possibility that there are *a priori* objections to a 'science of man' based upon the physical science model. But that this is in fact the case cannot yet be confidentally asserted. There are further arguments to be considered.

chapter 3

Causal explanation and rational action

One of the most influential contemporary proponents of the thesis
that the causal explanation of human action is inadequate, is Professor Peter Winch. He develops this case in his well-known book,
The Idea of a Social Science.

Winch begins his attack on the varieties of Durkheimian-inspired
empiricism by arguing that our concepts of what constitutes 'social
reality' settle for us the form of the experience we have of the
world'. He quotes with approval Wittgenstein's dictum: 'There is
no way of getting outside the concepts in terms of which we think
of the world.' Philosophical problems arise out of language but in
discussing linguistic usage 'we are in fact discussing what counts
as belonging to the world'. It is the philosopher's task to elucidate
the criteria of intelligibility appropriate to different 'language games'
which reflect forms of social life and to chart 'the conditions which
must be satisfied if there are to be any criteria of understanding at
all'.[1]

Thus, epistemology is central to all forms of enquiry and the
Kantian question 'How is understanding possible?' is to be answered
in sociological terms by showing the 'central role which the concept
of *understanding* plays in the activities which are characteristic of
human societies'.

As against the Durkheimian notion that the object of sociological
study should be social facts which are regular, coercive, general and
external, Winch argues that any assessment of the regularity of
social events involves reference to judgments of *identity* which 'are
intelligible only relatively to a given mode of human behaviour
governed by its own laws'. He reiterates Wittgenstein's question
as to what it is for someone to follow a rule, arguing that there is

no *formula* applicable to determine meaning or to establish that a man is following a rule since a man might always bring his action under the scope of some alternative formula at any stage of the enquiry.[2] Rule-following is an essentially social and *corrigible* activity which can only be understood within a form of lige.[3]

After maintaining that sociological enquiry is limited by one's socially determined concepts of what is to count as a 'regular feature' of social life, Winch further intensifies his attack on empiricism by arguing that forms of activity cannot be regarded merely as regular patterns of behaviour—they have a 'meaning' both for the observer and the participant and the meaningfulness of a piece of behaviour activity which can only be understood within a form of life.[3]

To speak *generally* of the causes of human action is for Winch to commit a fallacy which Wittgenstein exposed—the fallacy of assuming that the *nature of 'understanding' is common to all social relationships*. Nothing could be further from the truth, according to Winch. In two characteristic passages, he writes (p. 23): 'A man's social relations with his fellows are permeated with his ideas about reality. Indeed "permeated" is hardly a strong enough word; social relations are expressions of ideas about reality' and 'A new way of talking sufficiently important to rank as a new idea implies a new set of social relationships'.

To understand a society, then, is for Winch to participate in the form of life exhibited in a pattern of social relations. To grasp the point of this way of life, it is necessary to be or to become a full participant in the society for there is no *external* and *ultimate* check upon whether one has understood.

The cultural relativism implicit in Winch's analysis, together with his denial of the possibility of treating reasons, motives and intentions as causes of behaviour, has profound implications for sociological analysis, for what becomes paramount is not the collating of statistical data relating to regularities and variations of behaviour, but the act of *verstehen* which gives meaning to this data within a given cultural context. The act of *verstehen* is not merely an intuition which requires external validation, for the compatibility of a *verstehen* with statistical data does not prove its reliability. Understanding presupposes familiarity with a 'form of life' not coherence with sets of statistical data.

One of the major difficulties, however, in understanding Winch's position is to interpret precisely what is meant by 'a form of life' or what is to count as a bounded set of social relations. In a contribution to a symposium on Winch's book,[4] MacIntyre takes Winch to be referring to 'alien cultures' such as those studied typically by Malinowski, and Winch's illustrations do lend credence to this view.

On the other hand, Winch himself frequently refers to religious activity as a form of life. He writes, for example (p. 55):

> A religious mystic, for instance, who says that his aim is unison with God can be understood only by someone who is acquainted with the religious tradition in the context of which this end is sought; a scientist who says that his aim is to split the atom can be understood only by someone who is familiar with modern physics.

A 'form of life' then appears to be any activity which involves in some sense 'characteristic' criteria which mark it off from other activities and the successful sociological 'explanation' of such activities rests upon the degree to which the 'observer-cum-participant' 'enters into' this characteristic activity. A 'wholly alien' culture will then obviously make for special difficulties of understanding.

Winch argues that to pay strict attention to a causal analysis of behaviour involves omitting the dimension of meaning in social action. In answering Wittgenstein's oft-quoted question—'What is left over if I subtract the fact that my arm goes up from the fact that I raise my arm?'—Winch asserts that the missing element is the meaning of that act as constituted by the fact that it is enmeshed in a web of motives and intentions which are themselves embodied in a variety of complex normative structures. To understand human action is not merely to know its causes but to be able to *interpret* the motives or intentions of the actor within a social framework. Our knowledge of man thus becomes imbued with an *a priori* element which is ineliminable and beyond mere objective observation.

Short of being fully assimilated into a form of life under investigation the sociologist or anthropologist, however, wishes to give an account of the society in terms which are 'objectively' acceptable. Thus in explaining (say) the existence of a complex system of taboos whose 'manifest function' is to appease the gods, an anthropologist might well turn to an explanation of the so-called 'latent functions' of such activity in maintaining the power of certain élite groups within that society to manipulate others; or he might argue less plausibly that the existence of taboos was necessary to maintain the society as such, in the face of tendencies towards social disequilibrium. On Winch's account, if I understand him correctly, there would be no good reason except that of our membership of a utilitarian and scientifically-orientated culture to prefer the one explanation to the other. Indeed it might be argued that the participant's account of his own behaviour is likely to be the better since the scientist might well have failed to understand fully what the taboo system meant to participants within it.

This position seems so obviously implausible that one might feel that whatever the subtleties of Winch's arguments, the fact that they entailed such an unwelcome conclusion is refutation enough. But I do not think this would be entirely fair to Winch. One needs to distinguish a weaker and stronger claim in Winch's arguments and to reject the latter without the rejection of the former.

The weakened form of the argument is the insistence shared by most anthropologists and sociologists upon the necessity to take into account in explaining a social action the views of the participant actors—to understand, that is, what they conceive themselves to be doing in any form of activity in which they are engaged.

The stronger claim that the notion of meaning is dependent upon the prior concept of community is one that is absolutely crucial to Winch's view of social explanation. The refutation of this claim would render Winch's general thesis invalid although the supplementary thesis, that sociology deals in reasons not causes and hence is the study of internal logical relations not external causal explanations, would need to be shown to be false.

The stronger claim that concept formulation can be explained by a process of change in social relations involves Winch in a view of society closely akin to that embodied in the functionalists' equilibrium model. For if one once sets up a self-contained system of thought dependent upon a complex of social relations, conceptual change only becomes possible if 'accidental' changes in such relations occur through time. Now there is clearly truth in the contention that our concepts are at least partially determined or limited by the social relations in which men are engaged.[5] The notion, however, that all thought presupposes a language structure which is dependent upon social relations, that the concept of identity is itself uniquely socially determined, leaves us with as many puzzles about the nature of conceptual formulation and change as alternative answers to the problem which seek to establish a bedrock for the concept of identity, for example, in an intuitive mental act.

It is a truism that social action cannot be understood merely by noting or listing manifest behaviour simply because any given piece of behaviour (e.g. one's arm going up) may be seen under a number of different descriptions (e.g. signalling, expressing surprise, anger, indignation, making a request, etc.). But the conclusion so often drawn from this simple fact that meaningful constituents of human action make it *logically* impossible to explain human actions causally is quite invalid.

As May Brodbeck points out,[6] Winch and others trade upon the ambiguity of notions like 'meaning' and 'understanding'. Brodbeck isolates four senses of the word 'meaning' and five senses of the word 'understanding', claiming that they are confused by what she terms the 'mentalist' approach to the problem of explaining human action. Brodbeck distinguishes these usages as follows:

Meaning (1) is given 'When we know in any context the character or characters that a term is being used to refer to'. In this usage, the meaning of term is its *reference* established by linguistic convention (e.g. this colour is *green*).

Meaning (2) is given 'When the reference of a term is known to be lawfully connected to other things'. Here the meaning of a term is understood by reference to causal laws, e.g. the meaning of the term 'the pressure of a gas' is understood through its relation to other parameters such as the temperature and volume.

These two senses of 'meaning' are applicable, Brodbeck suggests, to 'scientific' discourse.

Meaning (3) is given 'When we understand what a thought process (or mental act) intends, means or is about'. We understand, for example, the meaning of the concept 'castle' or 'rain tomorrow' because we understand what the concept connotes.

Meaning (4) is given 'When the scientist investigates the reference (meaning (1)) or significance (meaning (2)) of terms or expressions for persons'. This aspect of meaning is referred to by Brodbeck as 'psychological meaning'. Meaning (4) is thus a tehnical term which

F

must be given meaning (1). E.g. 'fire' may mean (4) danger or warmth, etc., to X—although we all know what 'fire' means (1).

In conjunction with these senses of the word 'meaning' Brodbeck distinguishes five (related) senses of the word 'understanding', namely:

Understanding (1) is given 'When I understand meaning (1)'. E.g. in understanding a language where I must know the conditions for applying certain expressions and not others.

Understanding (2) is given 'When I understand "fully" or empathise with the feelings of others'. E.g. I do *not* understand (2) what it was like to be a member of the Italian Resistance although I understand (2) what it is to be the father of three girls.

Understanding (3) is given 'When I understand the meaning (1) of a term and also understand (2) the meaning of the feeling associated with the term or concept in a generalised way'. E.g. I understand (1) the term 'Italian Resistance member' and although I do not understand (2) what it was like to be a member of the Resistance, I understand (3) the meaning of fear, patriotism, anger, etc.

Understanding (4) is given 'When I understand the motives of other people (or myself) in acting'. E.g. I understand (4) why people are attracted to University teaching posts and why (say) people prefer to teach at one University rather than another.

Understanding (5) is given 'When I understand that one set of events is associated in some way with another set'. E.g. a regular churchgoer may understand (5) that regular church attendance means that he will be in a 'state of grace', I understand that increased costs of production will lead to increases in selling prices, *ceteris paribus*.

I now want to apply these distinctions to the argument under discussion with especial reference to the claims that a social scientist must 'understand' the society which he is studying and to the claim that the dimensions of 'meaning' present in all human action necessarily exclude the application of a causal analysis of human actions.

The sociologist generally assumes in his investigations that the understanding of a wide range of social action is possible for him in the senses analysed above. He assumes that it is not necessary to understand (2) all possible social relationships in order to explain what is going on in a society and to make predictions or guesses about the future course of development. Indeed the requirement that understanding (2) is necessary in all cases of sociological investigation makes nonsense of the discipline since it requires a fully 'empathetic' understanding of all the diverse phenomena which come under the sociologist's professional scrutiny. Hence the interpersonal testability of sociological explanations would become restricted to a very narrow range of investigators.

It is probably true, however, that a limited form of empathetic understanding (3) is given to an investigator through the process of inquiry in which he is engaged. In coming to explain the behaviour of diverse groups or 'alien' cultures the sociologist may gain new insights into specific dimensions of human experience which generate feelings of fear, loyalty, or dissatisfaction. This is perhaps especially true of historical explanation where the cultures under investigation may be not only alien in structure but distant in time. To explain the behaviour of peoples living in a Babylonian civilisation dominated by a fear of a multitude of evil spirits may cause the historian to re-evaluate and extend his assumptions about what causes fear in men generally. This *extension* of propositions about human behaviour derived from one's experience in one's own limited culture is part of the educative process in becoming a competent historian, sociologist or anthropologist. But the element of 'understanding' involved in this process is dependent not upon direct or empathetic participation, but upon a proper analysis of the behaviour of individuals subjected to a variety of social influences which are markedly different from those operating in the investigator's own culture. In order to 'understand' alien social groups, one has to concentrate upon the meaning (4) of various symbolic acts to the participants in that culture. To understand this meaning one is certainly not committed to the view that participant theories about the nature of their society are in any way superior to that of the investigator. The attachment of magical significance to human actions so typical of primitive societies is clearly a case in point and an obvious candidate for the application of some such distinction as that between 'manifest' and 'latent' function which grants superior validity to the *investigator's* hypothesis.

The notion of *verstehen* or subjective meaning much discussed in the literature, can thus be seen either in terms of understanding

(2) or (3) or meaning (4). No doubt, a series of general propositions about human behaviour is assumed in 'empathising' with alien cultures or in establishing what actions mean (4) to the participants.

Nevertheless, there is nothing special about such assumptions that renders them incapable of objective confirmation or disconfirmation in any given case. Let us suppose for example to take an extreme case that sociologists unearthed a culture in which fear was apparently unknown. One's first action as a sociologist might be to assume that the *expression* of fear in that society was either conceived in a way totally different from our own or that the expression of fear was totally inhibited by various social constraints such as legal sanctions, taboos or social disapproval. Nevertheless, intensive behavioural checks might fail to give evidence for these (and other possible) hypotheses.

In that case, one might be forced to admit a possible extension of the number and type of 'law-like propositions' governing human behaviour to include the concept of fearlessness—though such would be the oddity of this extension that such a proposition might only be admitted after years of discussion and intensive behavioural investigations. The point is, however, that such propositions could not be ruled out *a priori*.

In a similar way, a hypothetical Andromedan sociologist investigating the inhabitants of a tiny planet in an alien galaxy might have no concept of what it was to engage in 'game playing' or moral behaviour, for example. As long as the concept of 'game playing' or 'acting morally' had some unique behavioural consequences, it is not at all inconceivable that an alien sociologist might come to understand either activity, though he too might have alternative interpretations of such regular patterns of behaviour, which might be more or less valid than participant theories as to the meaning of such activities.

Obviously, in view of what has been claimed in analysing the concept of 'understanding' the associated concept of 'meaning' presents no *insuperable* difficulties to objective social explanation. 'Meaning' is not an inaccessible (necessarily subjectively or socially restricted) dimension of human experience. 'Cathedral', for example, as Brodbeck notes, is a term loaded with symbolic overtones and defined through a complex of normative associations. Nevertheless, its meaning can be made clear on the following basis: A Cathedral means (1) a physical structure of a certain kind and certain ways in which people behave towards it. Other meanings of the word involve the associations people have to it (meaning (4)), reflecting intentional meanings (3) or else meaning (2); that is its connection with other aspects of the culture, such as the economy, political structure, etc.

Thus, in each of the dimensions of meaning, there are objectively discriminable features which confer meaning on any term. All these features are in principle accessible to the sociologist without qualification. In order to understand the meaning of prayer, for example, one does not have to be fully committed to a form of life which gives unique access to the concept of prayer—one has only to see the concept of prayer in an admittedly highly complex social context, whilst allowing for the central importance in any analysis for the psychological meaning (4) participants in the activity attach to it.

As May Brodbeck puts it in a general context:

> The two expressions 'raising one's arms' and 'arm going up' differ in meaning in all four senses of 'meaning', referentially, intentionally, psychologically, and in significance. In this sense, as far as it goes, the mentalist's answer to Wittgenstein's question is correct. There is certainly a difference in 'meaning'. The relevant differences, however, can be objectively construed without appealing to vitiating participant 'inside knowledge'. In this respect, there is nothing about such terms marking them as 'logically different' from those of the natural sciences.

What I have tried to show is that Winch's arguments do not demonstrate that causal accounts of human behaviour are vitiated *a priori* by the fact that actors attach meaning to their behaviour and that of others. The relations between explanation at the 'causal' level and the level of giving 'reasons for action' are, however, notoriously difficult to adumbrate in spite of the voluminous philosophical literature on this subject. Argument centres around the problem of whether the so-called explanatory and justificatory modes are assimilable or distinct and compatible or incompatible and whether explanation or justification given in terms of reasons can be 'reduced' to causal explanations.

I do not think that any arguments have been adduced to resolve this problem successfully and by implication therefore I do not think

that the case for the *a priori inapplicability* of causal explanations
has been demonstrated in this case. What is certain, however, is that
explanations of human behaviour often involve reference to a man's
'reason for action' rather than the causes of his behaviour. Men's
actions are understood under the rubric of what it is *rational* for
them to undertake. In my view one cannot *dispense* with this
dimension in the explanation of human behaviour and to the degree
that this is so attempts to match a purely 'causal' model are vitiated.
I shall now defend this assertion.

RATIONAL ACTION

The so-called 'action frame of reference'[7] necessarily incorporates
a concept of what it is to act rationally. Typically, rational action
is conceived of as an actor's realistic perception of the *means* whereby
to attain his ends. I am said to act rationally if, in the pursuit of
my wants and desires, I employ the appropriate steps towards
achieving them. The goals that I set myself are held to be non-
rational—I choose to aim at what I value or desire and for these
choices there is no rational justification. I want to argue in this
section that the 'means–ends' distinction cannot be isomorphically
associated with the 'rational–non-rational' distinction, not only because it is difficult to assimilate all human behaviour into a means–
ends classification but because any investigator into human behaviour
is necessarily committed to the superiority of his own cultural
definition of rationality. That is, I shall argue that a commitment
to the 'rationality' of certain means *and ends* is an *a priori* condition
of academic enquiry into human behaviour.

Prior to an elaboration of this thesis, however, I want to analyse
what is involved in 'acting rationally'. In general, to act rationally is,
I assert, to make one's action in some sense congruent with one's
belief.

(i) Rational beliefs

Whether beliefs *per se* can be characterised as rational or irrational
is a matter to which I shall return later. It is, however, indisputable
that one can *hold* a belief rationally or irrationally. To hold a
rational belief is to have good reasons for believing 'p' rather than

'q'. What counts as a 'good reason' depends on the criteria generally accepted as constituting evidence for that belief within a particular field of discourse. Furthermore, to hold a belief rationally is to be aware of the procedures which entitle one to hold the belief and in virtue of which such a belief may be criticised.

What must be stressed, however, is the difference between the application of the concept of rational belief *within* a given discourse and the application of the adjective 'rational' to that discourse itself. Given, for example, that I accept the proposition that the stars influence human behaviour, it may be rational of me (within astrological discourse) to believe that people born under the sign of Gemini exhibit certain loosely-defined traits of personality.

Nevertheless, there is an important sense in which belief in astrology *in itself* is irrational in that it conflicts with, and refuses to recognise the validity of, procedures in other theoretical domains with which it shares certain common objectives. One might distinguish here with Jarvie and Agassi a *strong* and *weak* sense of rationality. To deny rationality in the strong sense is to deny that a whole area of discourse is both intellectually coherent and empirically supported: to deny rationality in a weak sense is to argue that wholly inappropriate and incoherent means are being pursued to reach certain selected ends whose rationality or otherwise is not for the moment in question.

Some caveats:

(a) To believe what is empirically false in an empirically-based discourse is not necessarily to hold an irrational belief.

I may believe (falsely) that an isotope of hydrogen does not exist on the basis of a scant reading of out-of-date chemistry textbooks. My belief is false but not irrational unless I persist in such a belief in the face of authoritative correction.

(b) To hold a belief truly is not necessarily to hold a rational belief. I may hold (truly) that West Ham United defeated Preston North End in the 1964 FA Cup Final, but base my belief upon the suspect grounds that whenever First and Second Division Teams meet in the Cup Final, the victory will necessarily go to the former; or I may simply believe that London clubs are by nature superior to those from the North.

(c) To hold a belief falsely due to a mistake in logic is not necessarily to hold an irrational belief.

I may, for example, reach a conclusion 'q' when there is demonstrably no connexion between the premiss 'p' which is alleged to entail 'q' and the conclusion 'q'. I may, for example, arrive at the wrong answer in solving a simple quadratic equation. Clearly in a case of this sort, I am in error. My error may be corrected by a better logician or mathematician and I may come to see that I have made a false step in the argument or calculation. *If this correction procedure is in principle available to me, I am rational but mistaken.* If I am too stupid to see my mistake, I am unintelligent not irrational. If I persist in my error in spite of acknowledging the general invalidity of the form of my argument, then I am exibiting irrationality. If I refuse to acknowledge my mistake and question the procedure whereby the mistake has been exposed either I hold my belief irrationally or I am a genius.

(d) To assert that a belief is held irrationally is not necessarily to imply that the person holding it is irrational.

Sometimes when a man holds a belief in spite of evidence to the contrary we distinguish the irrationality of the belief from a judgment about the man: for example, a man might hold Negroes to be his intellectual and physical inferiors. If he were normally rational (i.e., he normally held 'p' rather than 'q' when he had good reason to do so) we would tend to speak of his being 'prejudiced'. If he elevated his prejudices to the status of an obsessive racist *Weltanschauung* then we might prefer to label him 'irrational'. This distinction between the concepts of prejudice and irrationality depends both upon the *number* of areas which are, so to speak, infected by a refusal to accomodate one's beliefs to the evidence or the lack of it and upon the *degree* to which one refuses to shift one's belief in the face of the demonstrable absence of good reasons. 'Prejudice' is the semantic borderline between 'rationality' and 'irrationality'.

(e) A man's giving of reasons for a belief does not necessarily show them to be rationally grounded.

The citing of 'good reasons' for holding a belief cannot be an arbitrary or an entirely subjective matter. The very concept of a 'good reason' for holding a belief presupposes the existence of a community in which there is some agreed method of intersubjectively testing belief according to agreed criteria. To argue that concepts of rationality are culturally defined is in this sense correct. It does not follow, however, without further argument that concepts of rationality are relative to a given culture and *hence* are all equally valid or invalid.

(ii) Rational action

(a) To act rationally I have said is to make one's action in some sense congruent with one's belief.

Thus to act rationally as a juror is to bring in a verdict of guilty on the basis of a belief, grounded upon evidence, that a man is guilty beyond reasonable doubt; to act rationally in moral matters is to act in accordance with the principles one holds to be right; to act rationally in a prudential context is to pursue the ends one desires by the appropriate means taking into account where necessary the responses of relevant others.

Rational action in a social context is not merely confined to an estimation of the appropriate means to gain any given end. Contrary to received sociological opinion, ends themselves may be evaluated as rational or irrational. Clearly it is rational of me to seek my own advantage where possible or to seek the advantage of others without totally neglecting my own interests. It is not rational, however, for me to cite as an end the eating of a dish of mud (in the absence of a tortuous contextual justification). The pursuit of such an end requires special explanation in psychiatric terms. 'Wants' or 'goals' are not brute; they encapsulate a concept of what it is *rational* 'to reach out and clutch'.

(b) A necessary correlate to the understanding of human action is the concept of what it is appropriate to aim at. To be rational is to have access in principle to the canons for the determination of the truth or falsity of beliefs deemed appropriate or inappropriate to action.

This point is well illustrated by I. C. Jarvie and J. Agassi[8] in their article 'The problem of the rationality of magic'. They ask the question why someone desirous of crops follows up the planting of seeds with the enactment of a magical rite. What, they ask, makes the magic problematic and the planting of crops rational? Planting crops, they suggest, is explained (rationally?) by means of certain beliefs which show it to be conducive to desirable ends. They argue that magic is problematical because the belief that magic influences the growth of plants is incorrect or in some sense inappropriate.

The primitive is acting rationally only in the *weak* sense that *if* his beliefs were *true* then it would make sense to act as he does. Given that we know 'scientifically' that magical practice is mere superstition, we can argue that the act is irrational in the *strong* sense of its being incompatible with the canons of scientific enquiry.

The distinction between the 'weak' and 'strong' forms of rationality previously referred to can, however, be misleading since we may rephrase the distinction by saying that the primitive is acting rationally according to *his* cultural tradition but not according to ours. In allowing a weak sense of 'rationality' we are it seems making too many concessions to the thesis of cultural relativism whereby any action (it is argued) can only be evaluated and elucidated in terms of its own cultural context.

I want to argue that the primitive who engages in magical ritual is behaving irrationally although the means he employs to pursue his irrational goals might be appropriate. I do not want to be taken, however, to imply that there exists some Platonic 'idea of the rational' to which Western intellectuals have special access. But I do want to argue that certain concepts of rational action and rational beliefs are presupposed *a priori* by any anthropological or sociological enquiry whatsoever and that in evaluating and explaining behaviour in a primitive culture, for example, the investigator is committed to ruling out of court participant theories about the efficacy of magical practices. In similar vein, I would want to argue that the rational model of action presupposed in anthropological and sociological enquiry assumes the validity and superiority of certain logical canons.

Martin Hollis[9] in his article 'Reason and ritual' argues that 'some assumption about rationality has to be made *a priori* if anthropology is to be possible'.

He argues that the anthropologist must assume :

(a) that objects in the external environment have the properties which both investigator and subject perceive them to have;
(b) that utterances referring to the existence of objects and practices may be taken as *prima facie* true beliefs on the part of the subject;
(c) that the primitive subject discriminates among phenomena in the same manner as the investigator. (I.e., the investigator cannot merely make a list of behavioural responses nor can he *logically* guarantee

that outward similarity of reactions towards phenomena is indicative of a similar cognitive structuring of phenomena.)

Here it is not intended to dispute the fact that what a man perceives is in part at least a function of his language; it is to suggest that explanation is impossible if two people or societies have no perceptions or discriminations in common at all. 'The assumptions required', writes Hollis, 'for identifying everyday empirical beliefs are common conceptions, common ways of referring to things perceived and a common notion of empirical truth. Unless these assumptions work, the anthropologist cannot get his bridgehead . . .'

(d) That if the subjects reason logically at all then they reason as we do. (I.e. they must share common canons of identity, contradiction and inference which Hollis holds to be the 'requirements of something being a system of logical reasoning at all'.)
(e) That the subjects share a common conception of what it is for something to be a reason for holding or doing some other thing.

Given these *a priori* assumptions of empirical and logical consensus, however, there remain whole areas of discourse within which the primitive subject and the Western anthropologist offer competing explanations. I want now to turn to a brief discussion of the phenomenon of magical ritual in order to illustrate that the anthropologist is also committed *a priori* to the superiority of his explanations in certain key areas.

In much pre-Malinowskian anthropology, the preferred way of explaining magical ritual was to regard it as a primitive (and irrational stage) in the development of man towards the more fully evolved rational nineteenth century ideal. Magical rituals were just another 'beastly device of ye heathen' to be properly dismissed by tough-minded scientists trained in an essentially rationalistic tradition. The problem about this approach, as everyone knows, is that it incorporated a very dubious evolutionary view of societal development coupled with an arrogance towards primitive cultures born of the armchair critic, rather than to the honest-to-God field worker. But perhaps Malinowski's greatest achievement was not to expose the theoretical and practical weaknesses in Evolutionism, Diffusionism *et alia*, but to realise that the dismissal of primitive customs as irrational ignored *other* interesting questions about the relation which obtained between diverse institutions and rituals within the culture at large. 'Study the ritual not the belief' was a recommendation to begin answering a different set of questions to those asked by the evolutionist. The question was no longer 'What is the rational basis of the custom?' but 'How does it function within a given structure?' It is of course obvious that this kind of functionalist account does not *explain* the existence of the ritual unless a whole range of extra assumptions of the familiar functionalist kind about self-maintaining equilibrium systems are introduced. In dismissing magical rituals as irrational, the pre-Malinowskian anthropologist might have been a bit hasty—his attitudes remind one of the nineteenth century attitudes to certain kinds of 'madness'—but it at least had the virtue of raising the right questions. The pre-Malinowskian saw magical ritual as part of a permanent generalisable non-rational element within the human species; perhaps he ought to have looked for a latent rationality in the action in terms of its serving alternative useful social *purposes* which were not obvious to the unsophisticated savage.

However this may be, it seems clear that the anthropologist does in fact hold that Western 'scientific' culture is in principle superior in explanatory force to explanations given by an actor within a primitive culture about his own behaviour. The explanations given by a scientifically detached observer, however, are not necessarily true or even better than a participant theory in every case. Everything depends upon the anthropological competence of the observer in evaluating what is going on. Participation in the culture under investigation is not perhaps a necessary condition of giving adequate explanations of alien behaviour but it does seem contingently essential. The point is that only scientific accounts of (say) magical rituals are possible candidates for explanation. Explanations which invoke participant theories without qualification are simply not on.

But why should paradigms of rational action drawn from Western culture carry, as it were, their own logical guarantees in terms of explanation? What is it that makes such explanations 'superior' or 'more rational' except that we choose or are compelled to regard them as such?

A familiar justification of a scientific approach is that which invokes the twin deities of 'conjecture and refutation'. Participants' theories about magic are either empirically false or unfalsifiable. If they are unfalsifiable then their explanatory merit is zero. All methods of intellectual inquiry, it is alleged, conform to the hypo-thetico-deductive model. Hence, the absence of the possibility of disconfirmation guarantees that a hypothesis is non-explanatory. In so far as a participant actor subjects his explanations to the possibility of disconfirmation, he is being rational, so it is argued. Irrationality consists not simply in believing what is false but in not submitting one's belief to the canons of a generalised scientific method-ology.

A tough-minded relativist determined to save appearances, how-ever, might well argue that such canons were themselves products of Western culture and that no good reason could be advanced for preferring them to others. This familiar sceptical objection is one of a long line of such objections in the fields of ethics and epistemology. If one is looking for 'ultimate' tests and a 'fully grounded basis' for the methods of scientific enquiry then one is doomed to failure, perhaps. Nevertheless, the relativist anthropologist is in a difficult position coherently to maintain his sceptic-ism.

Anthropologists are presumably interested in explaining human behaviour in alien (primitive) cultures. To do so, they have to agree upon canons of explanation. In fact, some of them share the general canons enunciated above. Explanations are evaluated by them as more or less convincing. They reject certain types of participant theories. That is, they operate with implicit assumptions as to what is rational both in terms of means and ends.

Other anthropologists seek refuge from allegations of cultural bias by concentrating their investigations upon the *function* of certain rituals within the wider social structure. In both cases, how-ever, their arguments are criticised within a set of assumptions which constitute for them a professional reference point. Their behaviour and the explanations they offer are only intelligible within a general acceptance of what is to count as an explanation and what is not. Functionalists, evolutionists, situationalists and relativists all need to *answer* criticisms which allege that their explanations are not explanations at all. It is no answer to argue that one explanation is (culturally) as good as another.

The superiority of an 'objective methodology' is built into, as it were, the very concept 'anthropologist'. The acceptance of the superiority of explanations couched in particular forms rather than others is a necessary condition of his pursuing his trade. In so far as these canons of enquiry are peculiar to Western industrial societies, rather than to primitive societies, Western societies are, *in that respect*, both more rational and culturally superior.

Jarvie[10] queries this line of approach by arguing that 'savage *ignorance*' of Western science cannot properly be construed as irrational. Primitives, he argues, are more ignorant than us, not less rational. Jarvie, however, wants to avoid the relativist abyss by insisting that Western critical standards 'are better than no standard at all'. It is merely that primitives are ignorant of our standards; they are rational according to their own lights.

Jarvie confesses that his stance 'that savage ignorance is just as rational as civilised knowledge' is 'a very curious position' but thinks it preferable to the Rationalists' 'twinge of absolutism' towards primitives.

Now I have earlier both repudiated absolutism and argued that to believe what is empirically false (through ignorance) is clearly not irrational. How then is my position to be distinguished from Jarvie's?

One needs to begin with a distinction between :

(a) believing what is not the case (through ignorance) and
(b) being ignorant of the canons of enquiry.

Case (a) need not be an example of irrationality. I may believe that Betelgeuse is in the constellation Cassiopeia whereas, as everybody knows, it is in Orion. My ignorance may be *simple* ignorance, simple error. It is, however, eminently capable of correction.

In case (b), however, if I am ignorant of the proper procedures for validating a judgment or explanation, I am in a very different position. To be ignorant of such intellectual procedures and corrective techniques or to fail to accept the authoritative sources of such procedures is by *definition* to be irrational.

One must however also distinguish weaker and stronger forms of irrationality in the second case in the following ways :

(b1) No form of ignorance necessarily entails a lack of the *capacity* to be rational. A savage who regularly engages in magical ceremonies in ignorance of the canons of scientific enquiry may still be *educable*.

(b2) Ignorance of intellectual procedures and corrective techniques in the sense that they cannot be formulated by the actor or agent does not necessarily entail irrationality. I may act in a rational way without knowing *that* what I am doing is justifiable in terms of a complex set of procedural principles.

(b3) Not knowing *how* to validate my explanations is perhaps a more significant component in irrational behaviour but even here lack of know-how does not necessarily entail lack of capacity for rational action.

Irrationalism may be a product of incapacity to think clearly—either abstractly or in terms of seeing the appropriateness of specific means towards the attainment of specific ends, but I am certainly not suggesting that savage ignorance entails this kind of irrationality. On the other hand a weaker form of irrationality (which can certainly be distinguished from mere ignorance) can be conceived as that state of affairs where a person undertakes certain means which he mistakenly believes are appropriate to the attainment of certain ends and at the same time neither knows how to correct his behaviour nor is able to formulate the rules which might provide such correction.

Thus a member of a primitive society who engaged in magical practices in the belief that these practices would placate localised deities and thereby protect him from illness might fairly be described as engaging in irrational action.

It is perhaps the moral implications of the concept of irrationality which make us—following a principle of interpretive charity—unwilling to use it to refer to savage ignorance of sophisticated Western concepts and techniques of validation. In this we may be properly tender-minded. But neither moral scruples nor egalitarian sentiment can serve to disguise the fact that in offering an alternative set of explanations to those of the participant, the investigator is making an *a priori* assumption of the superiority of his intellectual world. Such an *a priori* commitment, however, is compatible with any degree of intellectual humility and willingness to attend to participant explanations.

In this section, under the rubric of enquiring into what it is for men to act rationally, I have sought to answer the question, is a commitment to a concept of rational action a precondition of giving an explanation of human behaviour? My answer has been positive but qualified as follows:

Yes, if by this is implied a commitment to the canons of scientific enquiry embodied in contemporary Western intellectual culture. That is, I have argued that there are implicit definitions of rationality written into the *activity* of scientific enquiry. This, while true in a perfectly general sense, has especially important implications for the so-called 'human sciences' in that what is involved in the given is, so to speak, 'infected' by the notion of the rational. The anthropologist or sociologist has, in virtue of his knowledge and training, access to truths which may be denied to members of the society he is studying. Thus his explanations of behaviour, to be 'professionally' acceptable, *necessarily* transcend the explanations of participants' theories. Given that many participant theories are inadequate the sociologist needs to *reinterpret* actions in the light of his greater knowledge. This does not imply that he can *disregard* participant theories—on the contrary they may be perfectly acceptable—but even in assessing their 'acceptability' the sociologist appeals to a concept of rational action which is necessarily both peculiar to his role *qua* 'scientist' and 'superior' in virtue of that fact.

The sociological orthodoxy, however, restricts the concept of rational action to that particular definition which attaches it only to the means rather than to the ends men pursue. I have repudiated this view for it seems to me that a commitment to rationality involves a commitment to the relevance of certain common features of human behaviour, to the superiority of the Western intellectual tradition as exemplified notably by the success of the natural sciences and thereby to the axiom that certain *ends* sought by individuals or groups may be characterised as irrational and in need of special explanation.

The appeal to what it is rational for men to pursue adds a dimension to the explanation of human behaviour which is not present in explanations within the physical sciences. The physical scientist is committed to the superiority of his explanations just as the anthropologist or sociologist is committed to the view that, *ceteris paribus*, their insights are superior to those of participant actors. The difference between them, however, is that in the social world understanding action depends upon competing definitions of the 'rational'—a mutual or one-sided decision to select certain reasons for action or ends of action as being appropriate or not appropriate to explanation. This, however, does not entail that all social explanations becomes 'relativised'—it merely creates a *problem* about the 'relativity of explanation'. But like the physical scientist no practising sociologist can adopt destructively sceptical views about the nature of his particular explanations.

chapter 4

An alternative conceptualisation: voluntaristic action theory

Sociological theorists have long been aware that causal analysis is in itself inadequate to the full understanding of human behaviour. Men attach meaning to their actions, behavioural contexts are often predefined and behaviour is characteristically 'goal-directed'. The 'intervention' of man into the world of social events as agent, definer or creator of something hesitantly labelled 'social reality' makes the behaviourist ideal already briefly discussed highly problematic.

Behaviourists attempt to ground theoretical discussion on a bedrock of neutral data. Adequate theory in so far as 'theory' is desirable or possible, is conceived as having anchorage in publicly-accessible data which are capable of unambiguous measurement. In many respects its ideals are laudable. Objectivity, neutrality and empirical reference, in so far as these ends are in principle possible to realise, are definitive procedures for the sociologist. Nevertheless the behaviourist programme defines procedural maxims in such a way that adherence to them by the sociologist or psychologist raises insuperable difficulties. First, behaviourism fails to analyse adequately concepts of intention and purpose; second, it presupposes or legislates for a relationship between theory and data which runs counter to the actual operation of successful theoretical sciences; and third, it fails to incorporate into its scheme of explanation the variety and range of interpretations implicit in even the simplest forms of social discrimination.

So-called action theorists aim to provide a perspective which avoids these difficulties but, as I hope to show, there is a tendency amongst action theorists not merely to insist upon the necessary ambiguity of the interpretation of 'social reality' and the 'open-endedness' of human behaviour[1] but to try to set up a general theoretical schema which can be applied indiscriminately to all forms of human behaviour. In trying to 'define' the concept of action or to chart its relationship to individual behaviour, action theorists have, in my view, been guilty of at least three major errors. First, they have rejected behaviourism only to incorporate into their schemes of explanation similar atomistic assumptions; second, they have taken as unproblematic the applicability of notions such as intention, voluntariness and the like, drawn from an essentially *evaluational* context, to the *explanation* of human behaviour; and third, they have tended to incorporate into the definition of 'action' illicit assumptions about the arationality of the *ends* men choose to pursue. In sum, the search for a *general* perspective on human behaviour has led to a gross oversimplification of the explanations deemed appropriate to human behaviour.

Talcott Parsons,[2] asserts that the schemes of explanation appropriate in the natural sciences are beside the point in explaining distinctive human behaviour. He writes :

> The question is that of the theoretical relevance and adequacy of the conceptual schemes of what are the 'natural sciences' for full analysis of the phenomena of action. There is ample evidence of the inadequacy or inconvenience, or both, of these conceptual schemes for this purpose and thus of independent justification of the action frame of reference.

For Parsons, there is 'ample evidence' that something has been left out of account in a behaviourist analysis. This view is shared by, for example, A. I. Meldon[3] who writes at the conclusion of an exhaustive analysis of the distinction between bodily movement and so-called 'directed' action :

> I have attempted to show that it is a fundamental mistake to suppose that the (causal) model employed in the natural sciences will fit the everyday explanations of actions in terms of intentions, interests, desires, etc. . . . . It follows that there is a radical disparity between those two models of explanation : causal explanations of events and our familiar explanations of human actions.

The argument is that the vocabulary of the behaviourist is fundamentally inadequate to explain human action. In explaining human action one needs to invoke *the goal for the sake of which* the action occurs. Purpose or intention is often held to be not a special un-observable causal entity but a dispositional concept whereby voluntary action is somehow 'exhibited'. Desires, ends or wants are not thought of as brute forces which *impel* the actor; they are seen as akin to intentions.

As Stuart Hampshire writes : [4]

> He (i.e. 'an actor' or 'agent') is not in the position of a man who reports an impulse or an inclination that has *occurred* to him as he might report a sensation. His position in respect of his claim to know what he wants is more like that of a man who announces his intention.

Sociological explanations necessarily presuppose the existence of social actors who are at the same time 'agents' in the sense that their consciously evolved intentions cannot be left out of account in an explanation of their behaviour. References to individuals' definitions of the situation and intersubjectively defined meanings are necessary features of any explanation of human behaviour, so it is argued. A 'behaviouristic purity' is, as Parsons notes, only possible if one maintains either 'a strictly biological frame of reference' or if one keeps 'the elaboration of the theory pre-symbolic or pre-cultural'.

What Parsons means by this is that behaviourist explanations can, in principle, only be given of animal behaviour. 'Behaviourism', he writes, 'really boils down to whether it is possible to handle the more differentiated levels of the frame of references of action with the precision and care which the scientist attempts to attain. As in other branches of science, the proof of the pudding is in the eating.'

But Parsons has already consumed the pudding, for he writes: 'It is a fundamental property of action that it does not consist of *ad hoc* responses to particular situational stimuli but that the actor develops a system of "expectations" relative to the various objects of the situation.' That is to say, Parsons maintains that the category of 'expectations', since it involves the use of symbols and norms, cannot be incorporated into what he regards as a scheme of explanation relating only to biological, pre-symbolic or pre-cultural events.

'Action Theory' typically sets up a model of explanation which incorporates assumptions about the way in which human beings typically behave. But the concept of 'typical behaviour' is not to be defined in terms of probabilities or other statistical measures. Rather it involves the notion of an ideal rational actor whose behaviour is seen as a standard case by reference to which deviant, non-rational or non-intentional behaviour can be explained. Professor Rex's[5] elaboration of this Weberian notion sets out a clear version of the assumption incorporated in the model. Any investigator of human behaviour must necessarily proceed on the following assumptions: that men have ends and purposes which affect their behaviour; that they consciously perceive these ends; that one can assert certain law-like propositions about human behaviour in general (e.g. that other things being equal, men tend to pursue their interests); that men perceive relationships of appropriateness between means and ends; that men adapt their behaviour to the expectations of others and that they employ the sort of logical reasoning which an applied scientist might use.

Action theory then sets up a paradigm of human action: it incorporates an assumption of what it is to be rational; it regards this pattern of rationality as 'typical' of human behaviour in the sense that men are capable of this degree of rationality (that is, for example, what distinguishes them from animals). The model has, of course, also to take into account possible sources of non-rationality. Human purposes and intentions for example may be 'irrationally' restricted by taboos; ends may be hazily articulated or metaphysical; the actor's knowledge may be imperfect or his 'logic' may be deficient (through madness or participation in a primitive culture).

An action theorist has to take up one of two attitudes towards apparent 'irrationality of action':

(a) either he regards it as a 'surface phenomenon'—he notices a *manifest* irrationality but assumes a *latent* rationality, i.e. he looks for a deeper level of rationality; or
(b) he posits a pre-logical mentality or a sub-stratum of 'permanent, generalised non-rational elements'.

The methodological point here is that on an 'action theory' base, there is a *prima facie* case for analysis in terms of the rational model[6] (although the danger of a culturally-biased definition of rationality must be guarded against). There is only a secondary case for analysis in terms of error, misconception or lack of knowledge.

Now in so far as the so-called 'action frame of reference' repudiates behaviourism as a fully adequate conceptual scheme for the explanation of human behaviour, it is clearly on the right lines. Nevertheless, there are concealed assumptions within this approach which make one suspect that it too may distort the nature of human behaviour. Clearly the terms 'acts', 'actor' and 'rational action' cannot be regarded as unproblematic. One must locate the concept of action within the wider framework of concepts, which relate to the description and explanation of human behaviour.

The central problem, I suppose, in the analysis of the concept of action is whether one can state the conditions which enable one to categorise a piece of behaviour as an 'act'. An answer to such a question, however, is not as straightforward as it may appear. The *identification* and description of an 'act' is in itself problematic.

Most sociologists, wedded to the so-called 'voluntaristic frame of reference', would characterise an 'act' as any piece of behaviour to which the actor attached subjective meaning. Thus, to go to church, to commit murder, to make love, to sign cheques would all qualify as 'acts' or 'action', whereas earthquakes, muscular twitches, behaviour exhibited under the influence of certain drugs or under hypnosis would fail to qualify, as would a 'mere description' of bodily movement. What characterises an act as such in their view is the direction of behaviour towards a subjectively conceived end or goal which confers meaning upon the behaviour. But this view of action, apart from other difficulties to which I shall refer later, fails to distinguish in any clear-cut way an act from the consequences of an act. If I put my foot inside the door of a church and participate in worship, then I may at the same time antagonise my atheist friends, acquire a reputation for inconsistency and hypocrisy, establish new sets of relationships with others and alter existing sets of relationships. Are all those consequences to be included under the rubric of 'my act' or is my act to be defined only in terms of those consequences which I successfully envisage in my capacity as a 'reasonable man'? In entering a church, have I committed one act or many? And what of my bodily movements and brain processes involved in my acting in the way that I did? Aren't these in a sense 'my acts'? And if they are not, what are they? And how are they to be described?

One way of answering these questions is to suggest that what is to count as an act and what the consequences of an action is determined simply by the context in which the act (or acts) takes place. For example, if I park my car for ten minutes unlocked, and it is stolen and used in a bank raid, with the consequent death of a police constable, my action is not culpable. I did not *intend* the consequences of my act and thus the killing of the constable is in no sense 'my act'. If, however, I were to leave my young children alone in a house 'negligently' when a reasonable man would have foreseen the risk of fire, I am to blame if they are burnt to death and am held to intend the reasonably foreseeable consequences of my act. My action in negligently leaving my children to be burnt to death may be redescribed as 'he acted so as to cause the death of his children' even though that was the last thing I had actually intended.

What this amounts to is the claim that any piece of behaviour may be seen under different descriptions depending upon the context in which the behaviour occurs and the interests of others in evaluating it—and here the concept of 'my intention' or the 'intention of any reasonable man' seems crucial in identifying an act as such. On this analysis an act cannot in one sense be unitary, that is, it cannot operate as 'brute data' for the sociologist since any act is embedded within a complex set of assumptions, interests and norms already in existence prior to the act which makes it what it is. Thus the whole notion of an 'interpreted *unit* act' appears self-contradictory.

Now it appears that Weber[7] was at times very conscious of precisely this point. He writes, for example, that action may be conceived of as 'either overt or partly inward and subjective' and that 'the line between meaningful action and merely reactive behaviour cannot be sharply drawn empirically'. The notion of action merely draws attention to the complexity of man's purposive behaviour in contrast to the over-simplifications of reactive models. 'Action' for Weber was essentially a frame of reference within which explanation of human behaviour necessarily operated. The notion that action could be incorporated into a *systematic* general framework was alien to his mode of thought. Even the construction of ideal typical models of rational action he held only to be a 'methodological device'.

In Talcott Parsons's[8] account of the 'general theory of action', however, things are somewhat differently and ambiguously conceived.

Parsons certainly conceives of 'the action scheme' as a frame of reference in the Weberian sense, for he writes:

> The underlying features of the action schemes which are here called the 'frame of reference' do not constitute 'data' of any empirical problem; they are not components of any concrete system of action. They are in this respect analogous to the space-time framework of physics.

At one level then, an action frame of reference is simply an affirmation that 'it is impossible to talk about action in terms that do not involve a means–ends relationship' with all the implications just discussed.

But Parsons does not rest content with this very general notion that human behaviour must be seen in teleological terms. He thinks it possible meaningfully to employ the concept of a *'unit* act' at what he calls the 'analytical' and the 'concrete' level. Parsons holds that it is possible to locate a 'unit point of reference' for behaviour which is 'the simplest theoretical term of all'. This unit point he supposes to be 'a system of action' which is an 'ontologically real entity'. The smallest unit of an action system which still makes sense as a part of a concrete system of action is 'a concrete act'. An 'analytical unit of action' is held to 'abstract elements in the concrete case and to treat them as conditional possibilities'.

Parsons's discussion of the concept of 'unit act' is characteristically obscure.[9] Let me try to disentangle those elements which are truistic in his analysis from those that contain objectionable elements.

First, one can readily admit that it seems impossible to explain human behaviour without reference to such concepts as intention purpose, rationality and the like. Second, one can clearly distinguish actions (concrete acts?) from classes of acts (analytic acts?). What is worrying about Parsons's view of action, however, is the connotation of the adjective 'unit' in his analysis.

Is it suggested that one can unambiguously locate, either concretely or analytically, some irreducibly minimum requirement for identifying a human action—that it be 'intentional', 'rational', 'willed', 'voluntaristic', or 'meaningful,' for example? If so, these assumptions need to be made explicit and to be defended.

It is my contention that the imposition of such a 'theoretical' scheme or perspective upon the varieties of human behaviour distorts the nature of human action. That is, I believe that the attempt to locate a basic 'unit of action' is misleading in precisely the same way as the attempt to construct a data-language. The action perspective merely denies behaviourism—in which case it is a relatively trivial position—or it maintains that human behaviour can be described in an *interpreted* language which functions in a roughly similar way to a neutral data-language as a basis for a *theory* of behaviour. The second of these alternatives seems to me to be ruled out by the arguments already adduced but clearly Parsons attaches some importance to the possibility of speaking in this way in order to build a systematic general theory of action. Perhaps it is possible to define action unambiguously in terms of the concept of that which is *voluntarily* or (alternatively) *rationally* undertaken. Parsons himself often speaks of 'the voluntaristic theory of action' but never of 'non-voluntaristic action'. It is possible that he conceives of voluntariness as a defining characteristic of action. It is to a discussion of the relationship of the concept of that which is voluntary to the concept of human action that I now wish to turn.

THE DEFINITION OF ACTION

(i) Is action voluntary behaviour?

It is perhaps more fruitful in considering this question to concentrate upon an analysis of the range of *distinctions* implicit in such concepts as voluntary, involuntary, compelled, willed, intended and the like rather than to range over the objection to the commonsense notion that actions may be defined in virtue of the presence of a prior 'act of will' or to plunge directly into the intention/cause debate.

Indeed, the flexibility of the English language seems to rule out the possibility of establishing clear-cut boundaries between the sets of terms involved in the debate concerning the nature and definition of human actions. If it is maintained, for example, that introspectable antecedent deliberation is a defining condition of action, then this appears to rule out of court alleged actions which are habitual and yet which in some sense we chose to perform. In learning a set of skills for example, success in learning is frequently dependent on (or is defined by) our ceasing to find it necessary to reflect upon our performance. Having chosen to want to drive a car, my habitually correct responses in driving it are not thereby 'involuntary' (although we might refer to a driver having an 'automatic' response to certain situations). Indeed, the words 'voluntary', 'automatic', 'reflective', 'intentional' and the like are used not as symbolic counters which have a predefined meaning but as words which mark the kind of *contrasts* we think to be important in specific areas of behaviour.

Let me list some of these contrasts with respect to some of the central concepts used in the explanation and evaluation of human behaviour :

(a) *Willed, willing, strength of will* Statements that involve a reference to an action being *willed* occur typically in situations where we wish morally to evaluate a piece of behaviour and/or ascribe responsibility or the lack of it to an individual. To will the consequences that flow from any given piece of behaviour does indeed presuppose either that one has consciously reflected upon the implications of that behaviour and (whether under certain limited forms of duress or not) 'freely' chosen them; or in a legal or moral sense, that one *ought* to have so reflected as a 'reasonable' man.

Thus, the somewhat archaic phraseology 'he willed it so' may be used to rebut suggestions that a man was not responsible for his actions or to suggest that he acted wholly spontaneously. Nevertheless, 'spontaneous' action may on occasions be held to be 'willed' even in the absence of a series of prior 'reflective acts' if a judgment is made that a man *ought* to be held responsible for his impulses in any given situation.

'To be willing' also involves the notion of reflective permission— but once again a prior mental act of 'willingness' is not always presupposed. A girl may be defined as willing in law even if at the last moment she changes her mind. Conversely she may be deemed to be unwilling even if temporarily overcome by sexual passion. What is crucial in determining willingness is not solely a state of mind but the whole context in which her actions and the actions of others are *appraised*.

'Strength of will', 'determination', 'perseverence' and the like are terms which point to the notion that some serious obstacle has been overcome in achieving what one wants. The morally obverse side of these terms—wilful, obstinate, stubborn—also clearly direct attention to the idea that constant reflection upon and holding fast to a course of behaviour is a special category of human action subject to rather different kinds of moral or legal evaluation than other forms of behaviour.

(b) *Compelled, compulsion, compulsive* Clearly there can be no dichotomy between a willed action and one which is done under duress or compulsion. In the world of purely physical events the word 'compulsion' is eschewed—a stone is *impelled* down a mountain-side; a man blown off a cliff in a high gale is likewise impelled, that is, what *happens* to him may be treated as an *event* in the physical world. Now clearly no decision or act of will is liable to save a man caught in a 100 mph gust of wind on an exposed cliff. In this case; the distinction between what *happens* to a man and how he *acts* is clear-cut. But most forms of compulsion cannot be so easily separated. I may choose to obey a gunman who is threatening me or risk death by a wilful refusal to co-operate and whether I am praised or blamed for my behaviour depends upon what is assessed as a 'reasonable' course of action in those particular circumstances. Perhaps in situations involving *coercion* we always have the opportunity to act otherwise although it could be plausibly argued that under certain kinds and degrees of duress no options are open to some or all of us. The determination of when duress becomes sufficiently intense for one to claim 'I could not have done otherwise'—and hence disclaim responsibility—is a notoriously difficult problem to resolve at the level of general principle.

What is certain is that there is no necessary conceptual opposition between 'being compelled' and 'choosing between alternative courses of action'.

Compulsive behaviour, on the other hand, is taken to refer to those aspects of behaviour where it may be legitimately claimed that options are not available. Thus, compulsive handwashing is taken as a symptom of a neurotic condition not under the conscious control of the individual. Compulsive behaviour is thus *involuntary* but not all involuntary behaviour is compulsive.

(c) *Voluntary—involuntary/intentional—unintentional* These paired terms are often used interchangeably. It is not altogether clear that this use is justified. Nor is it clear that the paired terms themselves are either exhaustive of all possible cases or mutually exclusive.

A voluntary act is normally contrasted with one which is involuntary (or perhaps in the more sophisticated literature non-voluntary). Thus, a paradigm case of a voluntary act is one which is performed in the 'total absence' of contraints (consciously raising one's arm as contrasted with sneezing at an inappropriate moment for example). Similarly, an intentional act is contrasted with an unintentional act in virtue of a claim that one has 'deliberated' and 'freely chosen' to implement one form of behaviour rather than another. Knowing what one is doing is a necessary but not sufficient condition for a claim that one is acting intentionally; I may know I am behaving stupidly under the influence of alcohol, for example, but I may not intend so to act.

But as previous reference to 'intention' in a legal context has demonstrated, not all intentional action can be construed as voluntary. I do not *decide* to endanger my children's lives, nevertheless, in law, that may be construed as my intention.

Intention is not fully analysable in terms of a state of mind; an involuntary slip of the tongue, for example, cannot be unambiguously referred to as unintentional; nor can one refer to unintentional behaviour as being necessarily involuntary. I may not intend all the consequences of my actions but those that I do not intend are not thereby rendered involuntary.

The language of volitions and intention is used typically where we wish to ascribe *responsibility*. All the terms discussed seem to have particular relevance to our *evaluation* of the behaviour of others rather than the description and explanation of behaviour. Indeed, it might be argued that the very concepts of 'voluntary', 'intentional', 'willed', 'compelled' *et alia* are defined by their interconnections in cases in which we wish to pass judgment upon others. Thus, in ascribing responsibility we look to some feature of a man's behaviour which we may refer to as 'intentional' but intentionality is defined defeasibly : that is, there are a large number of factors *the absence of which* leaves the action intentional.

The central point in considering the applicability of concepts like 'intentional' or 'voluntary' action to human behaviour is that one *cannot wrench such concepts out of an evaluational context and expect them to mark distinctions between human action and 'mere behaviour'*. There is no unique description of human action for such a description depends upon the meanings ascribed to action, in a specific context. In answering the question whether it was or not 'his act', we do not need some general formula but detailed knowledge of the context. We cannot make general distinctions between an act and its consequences for what is to count as one or the other depends upon our interests and evaluations. Where we refer to a man's 'basic acts' we do not thereby characterise or define an act in general—we evaluate what is to be regarded as central in a specific appraisal of his conduct.

To construct an example to illustrate this point: suppose that the sociologist is faced with the problem of explaining the development of defined roles within small groups. Most investigators of this problem would not give a thought to the elaboration of an 'action frame of reference' except in the sense that they presupposed that the voluntary behaviour of the participants was in some very general sense relevant to their inquiries. Typically they would chart the number and quality of behavioural responses which are held to indicate 'intellectual leadership', 'affective leadership', 'scapegoatism' and the like. They might construe what was going on as a 'system of action' in the general sense that the group might be relatively self-contained and relatively protected from outside (macro-structural) influences. But what constituted an 'act' within this situation would be determined by the particular interests and concerns of the investigator and the norms governing their behaviour and that of their experimental groups. Not *all* voluntary behaviour would be treated as relevant in these circumstances. Nor would there by any *a priori* legislation as to what was to count as relevant behaviour. Certain non-voluntary behaviour (i.e. unintended bodily movement and gestures) might be considered to be of crucial importance in the interpretation of behaviour.

The notion then that one can pick out *defining* characteristics of action is wholly misconceived. A 'unit act' cannot be conceived of separately from the particular circumstances in which a piece of behaviour is set. Human acts are data for the sociologist only in the sense that separate actions can be conveniently characterised for the purposes of investigation only if they are conceived as similar in defined respects by the investigator, his subjects or some official agency. It is no accident that investigations of suicide or religious belief are preceded by a detailed discussion as to what constitutes the data. There can be no *received* opinion on the matter. Action in itself is not a datum; it cannot be defined prior to explanation of human behaviour for action is both that which is to be explained and that which, in virtue of being categorised, has already been brought under some possible explanatory or evaluational scheme.

(ii) Does the action frame of reference mark a distinction between the types of explanation appropriate to natural events on the one hand and human behaviour on the other?

Finally it may be suggested that the action frame of reference, whilst not providing a basis for theoretical explanation, nevertheless serves as a useful reminder that human behaviour cannot be subject to the same kinds of explanation that operate in the physical sciences.[10]

Professor Hampshire,[11] for example, argues that an action frame of reference is a necessary prerequisite of the explanation of distinctively human conduct. He posits the existence of a power, ability or possibility, complementary to the notion of will or wanting. In the field of human action, argues Hampshire, 'X didn't do it because X couldn't' is a genuine explanation competing with the alternative 'X didn't do it because X didn't *want* to'. These two kinds of knowledge are distinct but mutually dependent and characterise the whole field of human action. In the latter case, non-performance of an act may be explained on the basis of the person concerned not really wanting to do it. Wants are conceived not as occurrences but as norm-ridden concepts of which the agent's report is deemed to be authoritative but not necessarily incorrigible. Intention, a notion into which Hampshire partially assimilates the concept of wanting, is deemed to be necessary to our possession of the concept of 'being in an active state' and, he argues, there is a special sense in which a normative element is present in all human action. He writes: 'There is a normative element in first person present and future tense statements about some states of mind and some types of conduct, and this normative element would not be reproduced in the description which a scientific observer would use.'

The key distinction in Hampshire's argument, embodied in ordinary usage, would appear to be that between discovery and decision—decision being a voluntaristic and norm-ridden term which is ineliminable from explanation of human behaviour.

Hampshire examines two classes of statement (two kinds of possibility) as follows:

(1) (a) *It* will not happen now
  (b) *It* cannot happen now (i.e. there are grounds for believing that it will not happen which are strong enough to justify the assertion 'It cannot happen now')
(2) (a) *He* will not do it now—implying a power of a different kind entering into our notion of 'freedom of decision'
  (b) *He* cannot do it now (i.e. he lacks the opportunity, means, etc.)

The transition from 'won't' to 'can't' in the second case, argues Hampshire, is altogether different from the first category 'for when we say that he can't do it we are not ordinarily saying it can't be the case that he will do it'.

In relation to 2(a), the question 'How do you know you wanted to?' as opposed to 'Are you sure?' is normally senseless, Hampshire argues. The statement 'I want X' is direct knowledge in the sense that it has no source.

Thus what men decide to do cannot be expressed, according to Hampshire, in antecedent causal terms : 'When asked 'Why does X want to do so and so, while Y does not?' we normally turn to the *reason* that he has for wanting to do so and so, i.e., to the place of this particular interest in the *whole system* of desires and interest.'

It is upon the premiss that a want or a desire cannot be given an antecedent causal explanation that Hampshire's argument rests. In fact, though, we do seek to give such explanation of wanting. The example of the man 'wanting a dish of mud' in the absence of any contextual justification is a case in point. Anscombe argues that we might as well think of such a man as a 'dull, babbling loon'—presumably because we regard his wanting as irrational. But upon what grounds? And does our concept of what it is to 'want rationally' thereby *exclude* us from giving an antecedent causal account of wanting in one case (the rational) whilst using it to give explanations in the case of an apparently identical empirical phenomenon?

Consider the two cases :

(a) I know what I want—a new car
(b) I know what I want—a dish of mud (to eat, say)

According to Hampshire, it is that in the first instance we understand because we see the 'want' within a system of interconnected desires

—and we see it further (and this seems to be an unwarrantable extension of the argument) as *evidence* for the existence of a non-evidental power connected with our action or free action.

As Hampshire puts it: 'One can intelligibly look for a causal explanation of a man's mistake in reasoning but the steps in a clear and correct process of reasoning *need* no further explanation outside the process itself.'

The crucial ambiguity here is centred in the word 'need'. Certainly we don't need to explain a 'correct process of reasoning' in order to justify it—it is *self-justifying*. Nevertheless, such an action may have an antecedent causal explanation. When Hampshire makes the claim that the question 'How do you know what you want?' is *senseless*, he begs the question of the possibility of an antecedent cause being given as an answer.

Certainly such a question is redundant in the context of ordinary usage—one would reply with 'I'm just aware of it' or some such question-stopping remark. But the mechanisms and determination of such awareness (in terms, say, of physiological, and hence, physical, explanation) might not be redundant in a different context. Why should a criterion of rationality which rests upon the notion of the understanding of a coherent system of desires necessarily preclude an explanation in terms of causal antecedents which fully determine the want? Hampshire's contribution to the argument concerning the possible replication (or 'mimicry') of human action via cybernetic models also exhibits the same question-begging approach. He claims that whereas a cybernetic model is dependent exclusively upon the appropriate input or stimulus, in man 'there is one *overriding* condition that must be known to be satisfied before the equivalent test of performance is accepted as decisive, that the subject wants or has the will to pass the test. If this peculiar internal condition is not known to be satisfied, failure in present performance does not prove inability.'

But of course, if one assumes that the concept of a want or desire is an independent variable operating outside the system on a relatively random or at least unpredictable basis, then it is tautological to suggest that a man's actions are no longer dependent upon 'the appropriate input'. A component of the input for man is the notion of what he wants and this could conceivably be treated as a physiological complexity in the organisation of the brain which cannot at the moment be matched. That observable differences of physiological complexity imply different *orders* of experience is one that might well prove to be capable of confirmation or falsification but it surely cannot be assumed to be true on the basis of an existing linguistic usage which cannot or might not be able to handle the problems or distinctions raised by such differences.

Hampshire's claim to legislate *a priori* in favour of 'intentional' rather than causal explanations of human behaviour cannot be maintained. Nevertheless, there is a sense in which analysis is an extremely valuable antidote to sociological scientism. That is, it cannot simply be *assumed* that the modes of explanation appropriate to investigations of natural events are those appropriate to the study of human behaviour. Perhaps the most fruitful way of representing Hampshire's case is to argue that it raises doubts about the possibility of providing causal theoretical explanations of human behaviour— doubts which can be substantially reinforced by an examination of the intellectual ambiguities present within much sociological theory. But one need not necessarily embrace an explanatory dualism in order to reject the *contingent* impossibility of giving theoretical explanations of human behaviour on the pattern of the natural sciences.

H

chapter 5

Bringing history back in: laws and the explanation of human action

I have tried to show that successful sociological explanations cannot be based upon models employed in the physical sciences, nor can attempts to create an alternative general and systematic frame of reference achieve explanatory success. I have argued that, as a matter of fact, attempts to formulate a systematic sociological macrotheory have either parodied the methods of physical science or distorted the contingencies of history in the interest of establishing spurious sets of causal or quasi-causal relationships linking dubiously-defined 'societal variables'. I have suggested that attempts to formulate sociological 'laws' invariably end in the assertion of triviality, tautology or falsity. But there is one escape hatch left open. For if the sociological theorist can establish that the explanations that professional historians characteristically employ, incorporate either explicitly or implicitly, macrosociological generalisations or 'laws', then he can construe his task as the *reformation* of the discipline of history—the explicit formulation of those general causal relationships which the historian assumes in giving an account of past behaviour. I shall now firmly close this hatch.

Although we may talk of trends, possibilities and limits we cannot foretell the specifics of future human behaviour. The possibility of alternative ways of behaving is always open to men. The interpretation of *past* behaviour or past events is another matter. Whatever the difficulties of gaining access to the past and interpreting the historic actions of men in particular contexts there is a truistic sense in which past actions are not amenable to change or re-creation. What has been, has been.

But cannot the analysis of the past give a guide to the future? Historical developments are not arbitrary or random, so it may be argued. History is not just one damn thing after another. A study of the past reveals that men both as individuals and highly organised groups respond typically to typical threats, inducements or pressures. Do we not in fact explain (or ought we not to explain?) human action in terms of deducing sentences which refer to the past or present from just some such set of general law-like premisses which can be taken as adequate grounds for the explicandum? Don't historians implicitly refer to 'the laws of human behaviour' in setting out their explanatory narratives?

Arthur C. Danto[1] has succinctly set out the problem of the nature of historical explanation. He notes that recent debates in the philosophy of history have centred around the following three propositions, each of which, he suggests, have some intuitive validity:

(a) Historians sometimes explain events
(b) Every explanation must include at least one general law.
(c) The explanations historians give do not include general laws.

Danto aims at an eclectic resolution of these three propositions, which, as baldly stated, cannot all be held to be true simultaneously on the pain of contradiction. I want to structure my own argument around these three propositions in such a way as to support the *third* of these alternatives in combination with the *first*.

UNIQUENESS AND CONTINGENCY

Every historical event is what it is and not another event. This is true in virtue of the fact that events are temporally and geographically located;[2] but this is also true of so-called scientific events. On 3 September 1939, Britain declared war on Nazi Germany and water boiled in numerous kitchen kettles on being raised to approximately 100°C under the appropriate conditions of pressure. Declarations of war are notoriously difficult to predict; the laws governing the boiling point of liquids are well-understood and predict well. Uniqueness, in the sense that each event is a particular to be distinguished from other particulars, is not a sufficient condition for arguing that such events are not governed by quite stringent laws. The 'difficulty' about predicting the course of human behaviour must lie elsewhere.

I have argued earlier that human actions cannot be defined in a unitary sense. There is no such identifiable thing as a 'basic' human act. Nevertheless, we do in fact identify and classify human actions according to our interests and purposes. Is it not possible then that given common interests and purposes, given a standard of what it is to act rationally, we might not be able to formulate laws which relate classes of action within a framework of generally agreed considerations which mark off some acts as more significant, and hence more worthy of identification, than others? And isn't this precisely what historians do? Isn't Hempel correct in asserting that historical explanation 'consists of a more or less vague indication of the laws and initial conditions considered as relevant and needs "filling out" in order to turn into a fully-fledged explanation'? 'Explanation sketches' in history might in fact embody quite loosely formulated 'laws' which allow of exceptions and extenuations. As Danto notes, when we are faced with the need to explain the lighting of a particular fire, don't we at least accept as a truism that people build fires when they are cold even although people's motives for building fires are in fact various? Isn't historical narrative dependent, as Scriven argues, on a tissue of interrelated generalisations?

The point is, however, how are these generalisations related to particular historical explanations? Is a particular 'law' entailed by a concrete description of actual events or by a complex explanation of events?

Professor Dray argues that neither Hempelian laws nor the assumption of implicit generalisation are necessary conditions of giving an explanation of historic events. He writes, '*in any ordinary sense of the word* the historian may use no law at all'.[3]

Dray considers the historical proposition, 'Louis XIV died unpopular because he pursued policies detrimental to French national interests'. He argues that the law or generalisation alleged to be implicit in making this statement, i.e. 'Rulers who pursue policies detrimental to their subjects' interest become unpopular' is of no value in determining the actual consequences of Louis' actions. He argues that such a 'law' is trivial in the sense that 'the farther the generalising process is taken, the harder it becomes to conceive of anything which the truth of the law would rule out.' Of course we know that, other things being equal, rulers become unpopular if they neglect the national interest, but what is significant in grounding such a judgment is the way in which this fact was exhibited in particular circumstances. Suppose we reduce the generality of the 'law' to 'Rulers who involve their countries in foreign wars, who persecute religious minorities, and who maintain parasitic courts become unpopular'—then the question becomes 'Does this generalisation apply across the board or only to late seventeenth-century France?' So many other factors—a bread and circuses internal policy, successful and ruthless support of initially 'unpopular' activities or the charisma of the king might have negatived the generalisation. As Professor Leff notes: 'To any practising historian, it must be the first principle from which he begins that events happen which need not happen and which could frequently have happened differently.' And this influences historical *judgment*. The statement 'Louis XIV died unpopular' is less of a presupposition of the explanation of specific events in the late seventeenth-century France as a shorthand expression which embodies a historical judgment in all its complex particularity. Of course it would be possible to reformulate the 'law' so as to read 'Any people like the French in the respects specified would dislike a ruler like Louis in the respects specified'—the 'respects specified' being a list of historical particularities. But then the 'law' would be vacuous applying only to one case. That is, it would be no law at all.

Dray also argues that there is a clear distinction between *classification* of events under certain categories (e.g. revolution, conquest, etc.) and the assumption that historical explanation must refer to implicit generalisations. Classification is undertaken not because events may be naturally grouped under *a law* giving the necessary or sufficient conditions of, say, the emergence of revolutionary situations. It is merely that one may, as an historian, conveniently employ the same concept to cover certain very general kinds of events such as the violent overthrow of existing government and institutions or even dramatic changes in social policy. Here the word 'revolution', for example, is a convenience. What competent historian would imagine that the use of the word 'revolution' in describing respectively an event such as the Civil War and the change in social policies after World War II in Britain ('the silent social revolution') was anything more than a convenient, and in this case possibly misleading way, of pigeon-holing events? I suppose at one level, any dramatic social change could be described as a revolution. The point is that dramatic social changes are set in contexts and require different explanations. The social 'scientists' attempt to list the 'general laws relating to dramatic social change' (and indeed in some instances to social change without qualification) lead to the kind of non-informative vacuity which Dray has drawn attention to.

Peter Rogers,[4] in commenting upon Dray's insistence upon the contingency of historical explanations has argued that 'we all know perfectly well in general terms what sorts of events earn and justify this title' (Revolution). He cites Namier's comparison and contrast of the French Revolution of 1789, the Russian Revolution of 1917, and the Revolution of 1848, as a case in point. Namier argues that the 1789 and 1917 revolutions were 'sustained by the converging action of the two greatest revolutionary forces: the (influential) people of the capital . . . and the (deprived and demanding) peasant masses', whereas 'there was something incongruous about the 1848 Revolution because the mob had . . . no articulate aims and no one will ever be able to supply a rational explanation of what it was they fought for'.

Rogers argues that the use of the word 'incongruity' by Namier implies that expectations of what constitutes the kind of events relevant to a typically revolutionary situation are implicit in the historical explanation given: 'Namier's explanation of 1848 is partly given in terms of what one would expect because the situation is revolutionary.'

These law-like assumptions seem to read: revolutions are character- ised by the 'converging action of the influential people of the capital and the deprived but demanding peasant masses'. The 1848 episode was a 'quasi-revolution' because unlike 1789 and 1917, the mob was 'moved by passions and distress rather than by ideas'.

Thus, any explanation of a given 'revolution', argues Rogers, is determined by what is the case in other revolutions. 'Comparison and contrast are given partly in terms of generalised considerations drawn from considering more cases than the one in hand.' Rogers leaps to the assertion that the Dray thesis 'by denying meaningful comparison greatly reduces the possibility of anything being explained at all'.

Now this argument seems quite implausible. In so far as certain events in 1789, 1917 and 1848 could be said to be attempts violently to overthrow the existing political order or to express felt grievances through violence by the mass of the people against their administration, all three might properly and conveniently be categorised as 'revolutions'. Two of these were successful revolutions; one unsuccessful. Their success or lack of it might plausibly be explained in terms of the lack of organisation and direction of the mob (though this reads more like a description of what occurred rather than the kind of explanation which would satisfy a professional specialist historian). Nevertheless, it surely cannot be a requirement of the explanation of all revolutions that they conform in significant respects with those of 1789 and 1917. The generalisations, if true, that Namier implicitly refers to in comparing these revolutions are still shorthand forms for describing what actually occurred. *But it might have been otherwise.* As Dray notes in another context, no set of circumstances can be held to be necessary or sufficient to an event happening at one time rather than another—or indeed, happening at all. Many revolutions have occurred in the absence of an organised proletarian class and a deprived practical and demanding peasant mass. No doubt also the *presence* of such factors has *failed* to lead to revolutionary situations.

Has Dray, however, fallen into the trap of seeking only *one* (vacuous) covering law, for a complex historical event? Are there not manifold law-like expectations implicit in historical explanations? And don't these different 'laws' conflict? Perhaps the situation is somewhat like that held (by Ross) to be typical of moral discourse. Perhaps there are certain high-level *ceteris paribus* generalisations which, in any particular historical case, conflict. The historians' task on this account might be to judge the degree of weighting to be given to each individual law. Thus, a whole series of 'laws' might relate to the emergence of a revolutionary situation. Consider John Rex's[5] suggestions. In any typical 'dichotomous ruling class situation', suggests Rex, the relative strength of the dominated group depends upon many factors. He lists:

(a) the strength of their aspirations
(b) their capacity for corporate action
(c) their numbers
(d) the degree to which their role becomes indispensable to the ruling class
(e) advances in technology with the consequent creation of new roles.

(a) may be sub-divided as follows: i.e. the strength of the dominated classes' aspiration is dependent upon:

(a1) the effectiveness of political indoctrination
(a2) the intensity of exploitation
(a3) the example of similar groups in other societies

(b) is dependent upon:
(b1) the quality of the leadership
(b2) the degree of organisation of the dominated class
(b3) organisational examples drawn from outside the dominated
class (including the example of the ruling class).

Rex continues: 'When changes occur in the balance of power,
there may be two possible outcomes. Either there will be a complete
revolution in the social system or some sort of compromise will be
worked out.'

Now each of the general factors cited by Rex as tending towards
a revolutionary situation can also apply to the emergence of what
he calls a 'truce situation'—one in which the ruling groups 'pay
ransom' for their privileges and where the dominated class accepts
the immediate amelioration of their position and the promise of
gradual long-term improvements in exchange for operating 'within
the rules of the system'. Thus, we can have no law-like propositions
which apply uniquely to the possibility of a change in power relationships for such propositions may be negated by other factors
or by the activities or forbearance of prominent individuals. Of
course, in writing of the 'causes of the Russian Revolution' the
historians are equipped with the hindsight and thus there is a strong
temptation to write history *as if* the antecedent general factors
determined the course of events which actually took place but hindsight does not give a deterministic twist to what was at the time a
highly fluid position. The action of the Kennedy Administration in
October 1962 during the Cuba crisis, for example, was explicable
after the event but during the crisis, as an examination of the
literature shows, a number of significant options were open right
up until the time when the final decision was made.

Of course, it may still be admitted that historians write sentences
of the form: 'The time was ripe for revolution . . .' filling in the
social and economic conditions which pointed to its possibility—

even though a revolution did not in fact occur. Special reasons are then given for its 'failure to appear'.[6] These kinds of statements can be interpreted in different ways:

(a) Revolution was *inevitable*—its appearance was merely delayed by the negation of one or more of the important necessary conditions for its emergence at this particular time.
(b) Revolution was the *strongest* possibility amongst a series of alternatives.
(c) A *superficial* analysis of the situation might have indicated that revolution was a possibility.
(d) As a device for highlighting what, in the particular historian's judgment, were the crucial sets of circumstances.

Of these interpretations (a) may be ruled out. No revolution is *inevitable*, even if historians sometimes write with perhaps justifiable hyperbole in particular instances just that. What is usually meant by 'revolution was inevitable' is that a chain of events had been sparked off such that no individual, acting on his own or in concert, could have prevented the outcome at a particular moment in time.

(b) that revolution was a strong possibility and perhaps the strongest amongst all—is of course a possible interpretation, but it involves a particular historical judgment and often a reference to a previous revolution which occurred *under like circumstances*. Thus, the form of the historian's argument might be: Revolution occurred in nation A in, say, the October of 1917. In nation B, somewhat later in time, with a similar social and economic structure, and facing similar general kinds of pressure, revolution, let us say, did not occur. The prior fact of revolution in nation A, however, sets up expectations that in relevantly similar circumstances the same crucial set of events might re-occur. Suppose they didn't—suppose one's expectations to be denied. This certainly requires special explanation. It seems to me, however, that this argument implies no reference to the 'general laws' governing the development of revolutionary situations *for the temporal occurrences might have been differently ordered*. That is, non-revolution in A might have preceded revolution in B—in which case one's expectations and hence the forms of one's historical explanation might have been quite different.

The third interpretation (c) is quite consistent with the view that historical explanation makes no necessary reference to law-like generalisations. Superficiality is defined as the neglect of important considerations which might have materially altered the outcome of an event. Clearly a vulgar Marxist expects revolution when competent historians do not and denies the possibility of revolution when the historian thinks it likely. This is an indicator of the superficiality of vulgar Marxism as a 'theory of history'.

(d) is perhaps the most acceptable interpretation of the historian's use of such phrases as 'the time was ripe for . . . yet . . .' backed by a detailed analysis of the particular situation. Frequently in writing of the complex history of interrelationships between different groups of different nations general expectations or intuitive assumptions are set up *in the minds of the reader of the narrative* which need to be qualified. The very point of using the phraseology 'the time was ripe . . . yet . . .' is to highlight the essentially contingent nature of historical events.

Let me now cite an example from Brøndsted's book, *The Vikings,*[7] to illustrate the difficulty of basing historical explanation upon the notion of laws. In his first chapter, Brøndsted asks the preliminary questions: 'Why did Europe permit the Danes and Norwegians to rule large parts of England, Ireland, and France, and the Swedes to form a ruling class in western Russia?' 'What inner forces led to the Viking raids?' To answer these questions, needs reference, states Brøndsted, to 'the centuries immediately preceding the Viking Age'. He then proceeds to sketch the political, commercial and social development of Europe at the time just prior to the emergence of the Viking threat but claims that the Germanicisation of conquered ex-Roman territories only took place to a limited extent. It was the rise of Arab power with its entirely alien alternative culture which led to the erosion of the Romanish culture in Europe. Only the Frankish Empire resisted. Brøndsted then poses the question: 'Why did the centre of gravity of Western Europe shift . . . from the Mediterranean countries with their rich and flourishing commercial life to the poorer, agrarian Frankish territories of the North?'

Now this question may perhaps be held to entail the following generalisation: 'International political and military power resides in rich commercial societies rather than in poor agrarian societies'. Any counter-example to this generalisation needs special explanation, it could be argued. Brøndsted gives as his explanation of the original question the fact that trade was inhibited or ruined by Arab military adventures whilst the Frankish society based upon landed property held its own.

Furthermore, the strength of Charlemagne's régime 'did not favour the Viking'. Nor did the political and military strength of the eighth-century *Rex Anglorum*, Offa of Mercia. The decline in the relative power of the Frankish Empire and of Mercian Southern England is attributed to the deaths of Charlemagne and Offa respectively. To present a highly simplified picture of the situation, Brøndsted's analysis might be represented thus as the 'interaction of various law-like propositions' governing human behaviour:

(a) International political and military power resides in rich commercial societies rather than in poor agrarian societies, *ceteris paribus*.
(b) International political and military power resides in societies based upon landed property, *ceteris paribus*.
(c) International political and military power resides in politically unified societies rather than those fraught with internal divisions, *ceteris paribus*.
(d) International political and military power resides in societies governed by able leaders, *ceteris paribus*.

The above scheme is, however, substantially complicated by a whole series of further 'generalisations' and specific actions whose presence give explanatory weight to the historical narrative.

Now each of these generalisations are 'true' in so far as they relate to a series of expectations that the historian or historically-informed reader brings to a study of the period. But the point of historical explanation is that *these general expectations can be denied by the actuality of events without causing one to deny their usefulness in subsequent explanations*. In what sense can they therefore properly be regarded as 'laws'? Rather than fulfilling the role of laws from which deductions may be drawn to cover particular cases, do they not merely direct the historians' attention to what might be *relevant* in explaining a complex series of historical events? Faced with the problem of explaining the success of the Vikings in establishing themselves firmly over the whole of Western Europe, such 'generalisations' direct the historian's attention to certain possibilities rather than to others. It is not an explanation of such events to argue, for example, that it 'follows' from the generalisation that where the power of one group increases, the power of another usually declines. We need no ghost come from the grave to tell us that. All hinges on the manner in which this generalisation is given historical life. And it is not the statement of the 'intertwining of general causal variables' which gives such life, for such a statement, if it gave due weighting to the influence of the vast array of factors relevant to the explanation of an historical event, would itself reduce to a complex historical narrative.

But history, it may be argued, is not sociology. In sociological analysis, we can afford to neglect the specifics of human action in the interest of establishing generalisations between *classes* of events.

As Danto argues,[8] explanations can only operate where phenomena are covered by a description and general explanations can only be proferred of those phenomena viewed under a general description. Thus, for historians, accounts of events which make great play with the particular, non-repeatable acts of individuals cannot be covered by laws. Charlemagne acted as he did not only in response to general pressures capable of being formulated in so-called 'law-like propositions' but in virtue of the fact that he was Charlemagne and not another man. To deny this is to embrace the *reductio ad absurdum* of Engels 'substitute Napoleon' thesis. But, Danto argues, we can formulate 'peculiarly loose' laws even in historical explanation. That is, we can establish law-like propositions of the kind that, for example, a country will always honour sovereigns of friendly nations —even though this generalisation is 'compatible with a whole range of qualitatively different events all of which satisfy the same general description and any one of which could have happened'. Such 'laws' for Danto permit 'creative opportunities' 'for the class of events they cover is open in the sense that we can, in principle, always imagine an instance covered by them which need not in any obvious way resemble past instances'. Perhaps it is the unique function of sociology then to elaborate such general laws which permit the historian to spell out the actual details of the 'creative opportunities' which were or are substantiated within the framework. As Danto poetically notes, an appreciation of the *details* of a sonnet is not invalidated because we are aware of the rigid nature of its form.

This notion of the role of law-like generalisations in historical explanation certainly seems more acceptable than the covering law model embraced by Robert Brown.[9] He holds that a combination of sociological generalisations—'an appeal to uniform associations between kinds of events and properties'—and statements of initial conditions in terms of 'specific events' is a paradigm of explanation both for the physical and social sciences. He asserts that the divorce between historical and scientific explanation is 'one of convenience and not of incompatibility'. But as I have tried to argue, statements of possible regularities do not function in historical explanations as do laws in the explanation of specific events or classes of events in the natural world.

In any case, surely there is nothing deficient, in principle, in our present historical explanations that requires us actually to specify the kind of open-ended 'laws' which, Danto argues, operate so as to allow for a restricted range of contingent variance.[10] Statements of open-ended generalities cannot, except in a metaphorical sense, be regarded as laws since their 'refutation' does not affect their usefulness in explanations of other events.

The role of empirical generalisations in the social sciences seems to lie less in their *generality* than in their claim to have uncovered new sets of relationships which are *relevant factors* in the explanation of behaviour. The complex relationship between socio-economic status and educational opportunity and attainment may be expressed in a series of stochastic empirical propositions but it is less *the form* in which the relationship is expressed than the actual relationship itself which is important. Historians have long been aware of such relationships but what has been established in recent years is their *measurable extent*—and the development of more detailed, empirically-based explanations of these apparently causally-related social variables. Major advances over previous historical accounts have been made possible simply because the sociologist is in a position both to *direct* his investigations more closely and because he has *access* to relevant data in a way that is denied to the historian. The sociologist who conceives his task to be that of providing merely general accounts of the way men behave is mistakenly perceiving generality as an indicator of explanatory power. In this enterprise he is still haunted by the spectre of successful theories in the physical sciences where this is indeed characteristically the case. One does not need to deny the great, perhaps overriding value of sophisticated and rigorous statistical techniques of investigation of the social world to

assert that the pretentions to general theory on the part of sociologists are likely to inhibit the development of successful, relevant
and disciplined explanations of human behaviour.

CONCLUDING REMARKS

Clearly not all sociological 'theory' refers to paradigms of explanation based upon the physical sciences. Indeed, the term 'theory' in
sociology seems to be defined either by the speculations of the 'found-
ing fathers' or it is regarded as a residual category—all work that
cannot be labelled as unambiguously empirical being classified as
'theoretical'. One can isolate at least three broad concepts of theory
defined in this residual sense: metatheory (which includes aspects
of methodology and the philosophy of science); speculation and the
employment of 'sensitising' perspectives.

Within the second of these categories may be included many
forms of speculation which are more or less related to the empirical
world but which do not attach to it in any clearly analysable way.
Some sociological 'theorists' engage in intellectual activity, for example, which is closely related to the tradition of disciplined speculation characteristic of substantive *political philosophy*. Ralf Dahrendorf's essay 'On the origin of social inequality'[11] which addresses
itself to the 'fundamental' problems which are alleged to underlie
more 'commonplace' investigations into social stratification is a case
in point. In reading Dahrendorf's collection of *Essays in the Theory
of Society* one is irresistibly reminded of the existence of an un-
broken European tradition of disciplined and imaginative speculation
which stretches back to Thomas Hobbes.

Again, within this second category one can point to a notion of
theory in which conceptual innovations and statistical evaluation of
data are united with an historical analysis. This *socio-historical* mode
of theorising is well exemplified in W. G. Runciman's[12] application of
the concepts of 'relative deprivation' and 'reference group' to a set
of historically-based but currently relevant problems concerning the
subjective response of manual workers to the facts of social stratification.

But perhaps the most commonly employed notion of theory in
sociology is that in which explanations are offered at a more or
less general level which are *compatible with, but not crucially tested*

by, *empirical evidence.* Merton's theory of 'anomie'[13]—offered as an explanation of conformist and deviant behaviour in American society —is a good example of this approach as is the debate concerning the relation of the (orginally Marxian) concept of alienation to job satisfaction. It is a feature of such explanations that their generality and conceptual ambiguity[14] makes their testing a very difficult under-taking. Characteristically the attempt to operationalise such con-cepts as 'alienation' and 'anomie' leads to a re-structuring of the range of questions to which the original theory was addressed and the relation between the operationally-defined concepts and the original speculative hypotheses becomes tenuous indeed.

Much sociological 'theorising' is, however, less concerned with offering highly general explanations of human behaviour than with *sensitising* the investigator to the subtleties of human interaction and to the shifting *meanings* attached to particular acts. Such *perspectives* focus attention upon the nature of the data from which regularities of behaviour are elicited by the research worker. The focus is upon the symbolic context of action and the 'background expectancies' shared by the subject and investigator alike.[15]

This symbolic interactionist or 'interpretive' perspective is offered as a counter-conceptualisation to the Durkheimian-derived 'norma-tive'[16] perspective which takes consensus about the meanings of human acts for granted. Disparate 'definitions of the situation' on the part of social actors are taken to be an *abnormal* feature of social life by the so-called normative theorists. The model of human be-haviour envisaged is one in which there is a necessary degree of normative consensus which is expressed through the operation of 'social forces', 'crystallised' in institutions and informal networks of expectancies which *coerce* the individual into the acceptance of certain social roles. It is the regular operation of such social de-terminants of action which allegedly provides a basis for the discovery of empirical generalisations and 'causal laws'.

These two competing 'theoretical perspectives' are not, in my view, necessarily incompatible. To the extent that meanings are shared by social actors the formulation of restricted empirical generalisations is on the cards; to the extent that social actors disagree about meaning or retroactively redefine their behaviour and the behaviour of others so generalisation tends to be more insecure.

Indeed the fact that the symbolic context of action changes over time has not gone unnoticed by research workers—the so-called 'ageing of indicators' is not just a *recently* noted phenomenon. The issue between the two schools is both metaphysical and empirical. In so far as the interactionist perspective denies the so-called 'determinist' bias of the 'social forces' model it incorporates a view of the nature of man; in so far as it asserts that shifts in the symbolic context of action makes the formulation of empirical generalisations contingently extraordinarily difficult it makes an empirically testable claim.

Now whilst I would wish to label neither disciplined speculation nor 'sensitising perspectives' as 'theoretical' I do not want to suggest that such activities are insignificant, trivial or pretentious. What I want to argue is that such activities cannot be regarded as substitute theory. In sociology there is a plethora of 'insights' and much validated data but successful theories are notably absent. If what I have said in this work is correct this need worry no one. It is just what one would expect. *Theoretical* ambitions are in a fundamental sense pretensions.

I might, however, be challenged on the grounds that I have so defined what is to count as theory as to *legislate* for just that conclusion. What I have shown, it may be suggested, is that sociological theories cannot match the theories of the physical sciences in predictive or explanatory power and this is news to no one.

Clearly I do wish to insist upon a relatively strict definition of theory but I do not wish to be drawn into the purely semantic debate as to whether or not sociologists who proffer untested and difficult-to-test or intellectually unsatisfying general explanations of behaviour are incompetent theorists or relatively disciplined speculators. The line demarcating 'bad theory' or 'inadequate theory' from 'non-theory' is not an easy one to draw. The aim of all sociologists is presumably to provide good *explanations* of human behaviour and the point at issue is whether all good explanations are necessarily cast or ought to be cast in the form of scientific theories. In my view, on the evidence available from a study of attempts to match variously defined paradigms of theory, it is better to opt for clarity, plausibility and historical and empirical accuracy in sociological explanations rather than to construct explanations which only parody scientific theorising or distort history.

But, it may be argued, this approach to explanation begs the question. Don't all explanations implicitly assume sufficiency in a full theoretical sense as an ideal? To cut off a point at which one is prepared to accept 'good explanations' rather than 'theories' is surely an arbitrary matter which owes less to the logic of explanation than to personal prejudice or aesthetic preferences? I have argued, for example, that the best historical explanations are adequate in their own right and that the fact that there are competing explanations of the same event given by competent professional historians is an unavoidable consequence of historical contingency. Nevertheless, it may be argued, historians improve or discard explanations held to be inadequate. Upon what basis do they so act if they do not implicitly adhere to the ideal of sufficiency as embraced by covering law theorists?

Two points need to be made in this connexion. First, one may hold sufficiency in explanation to be an ideal without accepting that its realisation is remotely possible where the explanation of human action is concerned. One may argue simply that the contingent complexities of human action and interaction defeat theoretical analysis —especially where the data are in a significant sense irrecoverable as in historical explanation. This view, however, is not incompatible with improving explanations where one can as new data are discovered or new concepts formulated. Second, there is no doubt that criteria other than the assimilation of data to covering laws are employed in the determination of the adequacy of explanations.

A sensible distinction can be made on contingent grounds between explanations which approach nearer to the ideal of sufficiency than others—between, that is, theoretical discourse in a strict sense and explanatory discourse in a wider sense. 'Theory' is distinguished as a species of the genus 'explanation' in that we can note a difference in the degree to which 'theory' more nearly approaches 'sufficient explanation' compared with all other forms of explanation. Our use of the word 'theory' in the twentieth century is inevitably influenced by successful explanations in physical science which have achieved a degree of sufficiency hitherto unrealised. Now it may conceivably be the case—and I do not wish to deny this on *a priori* grounds— that there is in fact no difference *in principle* in the logical form of explanations whatever their degree of adequacy. All attempts to

I

explain perhaps can be conceived as embryonic theories. The point, however, is whether this conceptualisation is meaningful or useful in the context of the development of a particular form of explanatory discourse. In sociology it seems best to trim the sails of one's theoretical pretensions to the winds of contingent possibility.

Notes

1 ORDINARY LANGUAGE AND THEORETICAL EXPLANATIONS

1 For discussion of this issue see R. S. Peters, *The Concept of Motivation*, London, Routledge & Kegan Paul, 1958, pp. 27–38.
2 J. O. Urmson, 'Motives and causes', *Proceedings of the Aristotelian Society*, Supp. Vol. 26, 1952, pp. 169–94.
3 See the discussion of operational definition in C. Taylor, *The Explanation of Behaviour*, London, Routledge & Kegan Paul, 1964, pp. 76f.
4 Ibid., p. 72.
5 I. E. Farber, 'Personality and Behavioral Science', in *Readings in the Philosophy of the Social Sciences*, M. Brodbeck (ed.), London, Collier-Macmillan, 1968, pp. 149–50.
6 E. Nagel, 'The subjective nature of social subject matter', in M. Brodbeck (ed.), op. cit., p. 34f.
7 Behaviourism does, of course, implicitly deny central state materialism. For an elaboration of this point see D. Armstrong, A *Materialist Theory of Mind*, London, Routledge & Kegan Paul, 1968, ch. 5.
8 H. Feigl, 'The "Mental" and the "Physical" ', *Minnesota Studies in the Philosophy of Science*, University of Minnesota Press, 1958, vol. 2, pp. 370–497, esp. pp. 382 and 428, quoted in J. J. C. Smart, *Philosophy and Scientific Realism*, London, Routledge & Kegan Paul, 1963, p. 68.
9 G. Ryle, *The Concept of Mind*, London, Hutchinson, 1949, esp. ch. 4.
10 Certainly this criticism has force against the dualistic theory of mind which removes mental events from a publicly accessible arena, but it does not apply to the doctrine of central state materialism which asserts that mental events can be publicly identified as brain processes or processes within the central nervous system. Under this theory, the notion of privileged access becomes a purely empirical question.
11 The steps in this argument are clearly presented in V. C. Chappell, *The Philosophy of Mind*, Englewood Cliffs, N.J., Prentice-Hall, 1962, pp. 2–5.

12 K. Popper, *The Logic of Scientific Discovery*, London, Hutchinson, 1959, pp. 93–112.

13 J. A. E. Silva and G. Lochak, *Quanta*, London, Weidenfeld & Nicolson, 1969, p. 63f.

14 See the last section of this chapter for development of this point.

15 C. Kirkpatrick, 'A methodological analysis of feminism in relation to marital adjustment', *American Sociological Review*, vol. 4, June 1939, pp. 331–5.

16 A. L. Stinchcombe, *Constructing Social Theories*, New York, Harcourt Brace & World, 1968, p. 56.

17 I. Lakatos, 'Criticism and the methodology of scientific research programmes', *Proceedings of the Aristotelian Society*, vol. 69, October 1968, pp. 149–86.

18 Ibid.

19 D. W. Peetz, 'Falsification in science', *Proceedings of the Aristotelian Society*, vol. 69, November 1968, pp. 17–31.

20 T. S. Kuhn, *The Structure of Scientific Revolutions*, University of Chicago Press, 1970.
    N.B. My charge that the 'rejection or acceptance of scientific theories are made dependent not upon the application of formal logical criteria but upon socio-psychological considerations' is bound to call forth the charge of 'oversimplification'. Kuhn's ambiguous response to criticism makes any evaluation of his standpoint difficult, but certainly the tenor of his 1962 edition of *The Structure of Scientific Revolutions* is uncompromisingly irrationalist.

21 Lakatos, op. cit.

22 I. Lakatos and A. Musgrave, *Criticism and the Growth of Knowledge*, Cambridge University Press, 1970, p. 113. See also a review of the above by K. K. Lee in *Philosophy*, vol. 56, no. 178, October 1971, where Lee defends Kuhn from the 'near hysterical charges' of his critics. He suggests that Kuhn's position does admit of the possibility of 'long-run' criteria of rationality; in the short run, however, 'individual psychology plays a vital and even necessary role'. I make a similar point in the text but it must be noted that such distinctions were never made explicitly in Kuhn's original edition of his book.

23 Lakatos, op. cit.

24 For an alternative view to Popper see N. R. Hanson, *Patterns of Discovery*, Cambridge University Press, 1965.

2 MATCHING THE PHYSICAL SCIENCE PARADIGM

1 R. Robertson, *The Sociological Interpretation of Religion*, Oxford, Blackwell, 1970, p. 3.
2 Ibid., p. 178.
3 V. Pareto, *Sociological Writings*, London, Pall Mall Press, 1966, selected and introduced by S. E. Finer, translated by D. Mirfin, pp. 3–88.
4 G. de Rosa (ed.), *Vilfredo Pareto—Lettere a Maffeo Pantaleoni*, 3 vols., Rome, 1960, quoted in the introduction to Pareto, op. cit., pp. 31–2.
5 Pareto, op. cit., pp. 31–51.
6 The validity of Pareto's definition of 'feedback' within the system is here dependent upon dubious assumptions about what is to count as 'normal' and 'artificial' change.
7 Pareto, op. cit., p. 31f. My italics.
8 Ibid., p. 182. My italics.
9 Cf. 'Non-philosophical unself-consciousness is disastrous in the investigation of a human society whose very nature is to consist in different and competing ways of life, each offering a different account of the intelligibility of things', P. Winch, *The Idea of a Social Science*, London, Routledge & Kegan Paul, 1958.
10 See especially P. Cohen, *Modern Social Theory*, London, Heinemann, 1968; M. Black (ed.), *The Social Theories of Talcott Parsons*, Englewood Cliffs, N. J., Prentice-Hall, 1961; N. J. Demerath III and R. A. Peterson, *System, Change and Conflict*, London, Collier-Macmillan, 1967.
11 See S. F. Nadel, *The Theory of Social Structure*, London, Cohen & West, 1957, pp. 144–5. 'If we believed in a social universe entirely characterised by the free will of all its elements we should not need equilibrium assumptions; nor indeed could we use them in any profitable way' (quoted in W. W. Isajiw, *Causation and Functionalism in Sociology*, London, Routledge & Kegan Paul, 1968).
12 For a succinct statement of the Parsonian position see T. Parsons and E. A. Shils (eds), *Toward a General Theory of Action*, Harvard University Press, 1962, ch. 1.
13 Ibid., pp. 21–2.
14 Ibid., pp. 22f.
15 T. Parsons, 'The point of view of the author' in Black (ed.), op. cit., p. 38.
16 W. C. Mitchell, *Sociological Analysis and Politics: the theories of Talcott Parsons*, Englewood Cliffs, N.J., Prentice-Hall, 1967, p. 185.
17 T. Parsons, *The Social System*, London, Routledge & Kegan Paul, 1951, p. 272.

18 R. Brown, *Explanation in Social Science*, London, Routledge & Kegan Paul, 1963, p. 117.

19 I. Lakatos and A. Musgrave (eds), *Criticism and the Growth of Knowledge*, Cambridge University Press, 1970, p. 119.

20 L. A. Coser, *The Functions of Social Conflict*, London, Routledge & Kegan Paul, 1956.

21 Ibid., p. 8.

22 See K. W. Wolff, *The Sociology of Georg Simmel*, Chicago Free Press, 1950, and G. Simmel, *Conflict*, (trans. K. W. Wolff), Chicago Free Press, 1955.

23 The accommodation is not claimed to be complete. Coser writes: 'To focus on the functional aspects of social conflict is not to deny that certain forms of conflict are indeed disruptive of group unity' (p. 8).

24 G. C. Homans, *The Nature of Social Science*, New York, Harcourt Brace, 1967.

25 H. L. Zetterberg, *On Theory and Verification in Sociology*, Totowa, N. J., Bedminster Press, 1963.

26 B. Berelson and G. Steiner, *Human Behavior: an inventory of findings*, New York, Harcourt Brace, 1964.

27 Zetterberg, op. cit.

28 This interpretation of the 'Weber thesis' is highly debatable. For a different view see A. Giddens, *Capitalism and Modern Social Theory*, Cambridge University Press, 1971, pp. 119–32.

29 The literature on the Weber thesis is enormous. A useful brief survey of some of the issues alluded to or discussed in the text may be found in Robert Moore, 'History, economics and religion: a review of the Max Weber Thesis', in A. Sahay, *Max Weber and Modern Sociology*, London, Routledge & Kegan Paul, 1971. Discussions of the limitations of the concept of ideal type also abound. See the articles by J. Rex and A. Sahay in A. Sahay, op. cit., and R. Brown, op. cit., pp. 179–83. An excellent brief critique of 'ideal-typification' may be found in D. Willer, *Scientific Sociology*, Englewood Cliffs, N.J., Prentice-Hall, 1967, pp. 42, 46. For a more extended historical discussion see D. S. Landes (ed.), *The Rise of Capitalism*, (Main Themes in European History), New York, Macmillan, 1966.

30 E. H. Carr, *What is History?*, London, Macmillan, 1962, p. 54.

31 G. Leff, *History and Social Theory*, London, Merlin Press, 1969, p. 47.

32 See note 29 for references.

33 J. T. McNeill, *The History and Character of Calvinism*, Oxford University Press, 1954.

34 H. Thomson-Kerr (ed.), *A Compendium of the Institutes of Christian Religion* (J. Calvin), Philadelphia, Ambassador Books, 1939.

3 CAUSAL EXPLANATION AND RATIONAL ACTION

1 P. Winch, *The Idea of a Social Science*, London, Routledge & Kegan Paul, 1958.
2 That is, the concept of what is to count as 'identical' phenomena is learnt in a social context.
3 'What has to be accepted, the given, so one could say is forms of life.' L. Wittgenstein, *Philosophical Investigations*, London, Blackwell, 1951, part II, xi, p. 226.
4 A. MacIntyre and D. Bell, 'The idea of a social science' (Symposium), *Proceedings of the Aristotelian Society*, Supp. Vol. 41, July 1967.
5 If this were not so, then the sociology of knowledge would not be possible.
6 M. Brodbeck, 'Meaning and action' in M. Brodbeck (ed.), *Readings in the Philosophy of the Social Sciences*, London, Collier-Macmillan, 1968.
7 See chapter 4.
8 I. C. Jarvie and J. Agassi, 'The problem of the rationality of magic', *British Journal of Sociology*, 1967, pp. 55–74.
9 M. Hollis, 'Reason and ritual', *Philosophy*, July 1968, vol. 43, no. 165.
10 I. C. Jarvie, *The Revolution in Anthropology*, London, Routledge & Kegan Paul, 1964, ch. 5.

4 AN ALTERNATIVE CONCEPTUALISATION: VOLUNTARISTIC ACTION THEORY

1 I refer here to an extensive literature which opposes sociological scientism in the interests of advocating a 'humanistic' sociology. Within this school of 'symbolic interactionism'—a general category which includes 'theorists' such as Simmel, G. H. Mead, Kenneth Burke, Herbert Blumer, Peter Berger and arguably the ethnomethodologists— the interpretation of the concept of action avoids most of the difficulties I refer to in the text. The action frame of reference is employed, in their view, merely as a way of sensitising sociologists to the symbolic complexity and processual nature of human interaction. As Arthur Brittan remarks of sociology in his *Meanings and Situations*, Routledge & Kegan Paul, 1973, ch. 1 : 'It is humanistic; which is to say its focus of interest lies in the symbolic and meaningful aspects of social action. It therefore accepts that the inner world of intention, motive and attitude is the proper subject matter of sociology—it constitutes the reservoir of social facts.'

Brittan's point is that the action frame of reference does not provide a systematic general framework; rather it acts as a reminder to scientistically-inclined sociologists that the facts of consciousness, purpose and choice between 'real' alternatives are central to an analysis of human behaviour. Precisely how the subjective definitions and discriminations of the actor relate to his behaviour towards others in a social setting is the central task to which the symbolic interactionist addresses himself.

2 Talcott Parsons, *The Social System*, London, Routledge & Kegan Paul, 1951, p. 541.

3 A. I. Meldon, *Free Action*, London, Routledge & Kegan Paul, 1961.

4 S. Hampshire, *Freedom of the Individual*, London, Chatto & Windus, 1965.

5 J. Rex, *Key Problems of Sociological Theory*, London, Routledge & Kegan Paul, 1961, ch. 19.

6 There are significant differences here between Parsons and Weber. See T. Parsons, *The Structure of Social Action*, Chicago, Free Press, 1949.

7 M. Weber, *The Theory of Social Economic Organisation* (ed. T. Parsons), Chicago, Free Press, 1957, pp. 88–100.

8 T. Parsons, op. cit., p. 733 (see p. 6).

9 In fact the concept of the unit act tends to disappear or remain submerged in Parsons's later work after its initial formulation in *The Structure of Social Action*.

10 This has always been a central issue in the philosophy of the social sciences. See, for example, Dilthey's elaboration of the distinction between 'natural science' (*Naturwissenschaft*) and 'the study of cultural and social behaviour' (*Geisteswissenschaft*). Ref. H. A. Hodges, *The Philosophy of Wilhelm Dilthey*, London, Routledge & Kegan Paul, 1952.

11 S. Hampshire, op. cit.

5   BRINGING HISTORY BACK IN: LAWS AND THE EXPLANATION OF HUMAN ACTION

1 A. C. Danto, *Analytic Philosophy of History*, Cambridge University Press, 1968, p. 203f.

2 No action can be, in one sense, unique since its description involves reference to other actions or possible actions.

3 My italics. Note that within the literature the status of covering laws is ambiguous. Hempel defines such a law as 'a statement of universal conditional form which is capable of being confirmed or disconfirmed' but he allows for the possibility of 'probability hypotheses' functioning as laws. Gardiner speaks of laws as generalisations, rules or general

hypotheticals. Scriven and Popper refer to *trivial* generalisations but the former views their role as 'justificatory' whilst the latter considers them to be premisses from which deductions can be made.

See C. G. Hempel, 'The function of general laws in history', reprinted in P. Gardiner (ed.), *Theories of History*, Chicago, Free Press, 1959, pp. 344–56; P. Gardiner, *The Nature of Historical Explanation*, Oxford University Press, 1952; M. Scriven, 'Truisms as the grounds for historical explanation', in Gardiner, op. cit.; K. R. Popper, *The Poverty of Historicism*, London, Routledge & Kegan Paul, 1957; W. Dray, *Laws and Explanation in History*, London, Oxford University Press, 1957; R. F. Atkinson, Explanation in history, *Proceedings of the Aristotelian Society*, May 1972.

4 P. Rogers, 'History', in K. Dixon (ed.), *Philosophy of Education and the Curriculum*, Pergamon Press, 1972.

5 J. Rex, *Key Problems in Sociological Theory*, London, Routledge & Kegan Paul, 1961.

6 See H. Stretton, *The Political Sciences*, London, Routledge & Kegan Paul, 1969, ch. 1.

7 J. Brøndsted, *The Vikings*, Pelican Books, 1970 ed.

8 Arthur C. Danto, *Analytic Philosophy of History*, Cambridge University Press, 1968, p. 226.

9 R. Brown, *Explanation in the Social Sciences*, London, Routledge & Kegan Paul, 1963.

10 I say 'in principle' although of course much historical 'explanation' involves the use of such dubious concepts as 'national character' or attaches too much weight to the influences of 'key' personages. The fact that history is not *just* about 'kings and ministers' in no way goes to show that the 'accidental' actions of individuals are irrelevant.

11 R. Dahrendorf, 'On the origin of social inequality among men' in R. Dahrendorf, *Essays in the Theory of Society*, London, Routledge & Kegan Paul, 1968.

12 W. G. Runciman, *Relative Deprivation and Social Justice*, London, Routledge & Kegan Paul, 1966.

13 R. K. Merton, *Social Theory and Social Structure*, Chicago, Free Press, 1957.

14 S. Lukes, 'Alienation and anomie', in P. Laslett and W. G. Runciman (eds), *Philosophy, Politics and Society*, 3rd series, Oxford, Blackwell, 1967.

15 The literature is voluminous. A good introductory reader is A. Rose (ed.), *Human Behaviour and Social Processes*, London, Routledge & Kegan Paul, 1962. See also: T. P. Wilson, 'Conceptions of interaction and forms of sociological explanation', *American Sociological Review*,

vol. 35, no. 4, August 1970. The article also contains a useful bibliography.

The classic work is undoubtedly G. H. Mead, *Mind, Self and Society* (ed. C. W. Morris), University of Chicago Press, 1934.

For a closely allied viewpoint see H. Garfinkel, *Studies in Ethnomethodology*, Englewood Cliffs, N.J., Prentice-Hall, 1967.

16 E. Durkheim, *Rules of Sociological Method* (ed. G. E. C. Catlin), Chicago, Free Press, 1938, and E. Durkheim, *Suicide*, London, Routledge & Kegan Paul, 1952.

action, 14, 76, 88–103
  and reaction, 43
  logical, 33
  non-logical, 33
  principles of, 43
  rational, 67, 76–87
Agassi, J., 77–9
  and Jarvie, I. C., 77, 79
  aggression, 49
  anomie, 117
  asceticism, 62
  axioms, 57f

bedrock, empirical, 8, 9, 12
behaviourism, 5–8, 88
  methodological, 6
  philosophical, 6
Berelson, B. and Steiner, G., 53, 55
black body problem, 12
Black, M., 44
Brodbeck, M., 71–5
Brøndsted, J., 112
Brown, R., 44
brute fact, 8

Calvin, John, 60–6
Carr, E. H., 60
Cartesianism, 7, 8
causal, 28
  accounts, 67
  problem, 27, 59
compulsion, 97
conditions, 28
conflict, social, 44–51
  consensus debate, 51
congruence, 61, 62

contingency, 105f
Coser, L. A., 44–52

Dahrendorf, R., 116
Danto, A. C., 105, 114
data language, 5–14
definition of the situation, 117
derivations, 34f
Devereux, E., 41, 44
dispositions, 1, 2
Dray, W., 106, 107
dualism, explanatory, 103
duelling, 49
Durkheim, E., 67, 117
dyad, 51

economic man, 54
elect, 63
empiricism, vii, 7, 10
environment, external, 41
equilibrium, 30, 42, 52
  as : interdependence (i), 41f
      homeostasis (ii), 41f
      ideal laws (iii), 41f
      stable reciprocities (iv), 41f
  concrete, 32
  dynamic, 40
  mechanical, 31
  theoretical, 32
exchange theory, 54
experiments, crucial, 15, 17
explanation, 1–3
  historical, 104–16

falsification, 14, 15
Farber, I. E., 6

International Library of Sociology

Edited by
John Rex
University of Warwick

Founded by
Karl Mannheim

as The International Library of Sociology
and Social Reconstruction

*This Catalogue also contains other Social Science
series published by Routledge*

Routledge & Kegan Paul   London and Boston

68-74 Carter Lane London EC4V 5EL
9 Park Street Boston Mass 02108

Contents

● *Books so marked are available in paperback*
All books are in Metric Demy 8vo format (216 × 138mm approx.)

GENERAL SOCIOLOGY

Belshaw, Cyril. The Conditions of Social Performance. *An Exploratory Theory. 144 pp.*

Brown, Robert. Explanation in Social Science. *208 pp.*

● Rules and Laws in Sociology.

Cain, Maureen E. Society and the Policeman's Role. *About 300 pp.*

Gibson, Quentin. The Logic of Social Enquiry. *240 pp.*

Gurvitch, Georges. Sociology of Law. *Preface by Roscoe Pound. 264 pp.*

Homans, George C. Sentiments and Activities: *Essays in Social Science. 336 pp.*

Johnson, Harry M. Sociology: *a Systematic Introduction. Foreword by Robert K. Merton. 710 pp.*

Mannheim, Karl. Essays on Sociology and Social Psychology. *Edited by Paul Keckskemeti. With Editorial Note by Adolph Lowe. 344 pp.*

Systematic Sociology: *An Introduction to the Study of Society. Edited by J. S. Erös and Professor W. A. C. Stewart. 220 pp.*

Martindale, Don. The Nature and Types of Sociological Theory. *292 pp.*

● **Maus, Heinz.** A Short History of Sociology. *234 pp.*

Mey, Harald. Field-Theory. *A Study of its Application in the Social Sciences. 352 pp.*

Myrdal, Gunnar. Value in Social Theory: *A Collection of Essays on Methodology. Edited by Paul Streeten. 332 pp.*

Ogburn, William F., and **Nimkoff, Meyer F.** A Handbook of Sociology. *Preface by Karl Mannheim. 656 pp. 46 figures. 35 tables.*

Parsons, Talcott, and **Smelser, Neil J.** Economy and Society: *A Study in the Integration of Economic and Social Theory. 362 pp.*

● **Rex, John.** Key Problems of Sociological Theory. *220 pp.*

Urry, John. Reference Groups and the Theory of Revolution.

FOREIGN CLASSICS OF SOCIOLOGY

● **Durkheim, Emile.** Suicide. *A Study in Sociology. Edited and with an Introduction by George Simpson. 404 pp.*

Professional Ethics and Civic Morals. *Translated by Cornelia Brookfield. 288 pp.*

● **Gerth, H. H.,** and **Mills, C. Wright.** From Max Weber: *Essays in Sociology. 502 pp.*

Tönnies, Ferdinand. Community and Association. *(Gemeinschaft und Gesellschaft.) Translated and Supplemented by Charles P. Loomis. Foreword by Pitirim A. Sorokin. 334 pp.*

SOCIAL STRUCTURE

Andreski, Stanislav. Military Organization and Society. *Foreword by Professor A. R. Radcliffe-Brown. 226 pp. 1 folder.*

Coontz, Sydney H. Population Theories and the Economic Interpretation. *202 pp.*

Coser, Lewis. The Functions of Social Conflict. *204 pp.*

Dickie-Clark, H. F. Marginal Situation: *A Sociological Study of a Coloured Group. 240 pp. 11 tables.*

Glass, D. V. (Ed.). Social Mobility in Britain. *Contributions by J. Berent, T. Bottomore, R. C. Chambers, J. Floud, D. V. Glass, J. R. Hall, H. T. Himmelweit, R. K. Kelsall, F. M. Martin, C. A. Moser, R. Mukherjee, and W. Ziegel. 420 pp.*

Glaser, Barney, and **Strauss, Anselm L.** Status Passage. *A Formal Theory. 208 pp.*

Jones, Garth N. Planned Organizational Change: *An Exploratory Study Using an Empirical Approach. 268 pp.*

Kelsall, R. K. Higher Civil Servants in Britain: *From 1870 to the Present Day. 268 pp. 31 tables.*

König, René. The Community. *232 pp. Illustrated.*

● **Lawton, Denis.** Social Class, Language and Education. *192 pp.*

McLeish, John. The Theory of Social Change: *Four Views Considered. 128 pp.*

Marsh, David C. The Changing Social Structure of England and Wales, 1871-1961. *288 pp.*

Mouzelis, Nicos. Organization and Bureaucracy. *An Analysis of Modern Theories. 240 pp.*

Mulkay, M. J. Functionalism, Exchange and Theoretical Strategy. *272 pp.*

Ossowski, Stanislaw. Class Structure in the Social Consciousness. *210 pp.*

SOCIOLOGY AND POLITICS

Hertz, Frederick. Nationality in History and Politics: *A Psychology and Sociology of National Sentiment and Nationalism. 432 pp.*

Kornhauser, William. The Politics of Mass Society. *272 pp. 20 tables.*

Laidler, Harry W. History of Socialism. *Social-Economic Movements: An Historical and Comparative Survey of Socialism, Communism, Co-operation, Utopianism; and other Systems of Reform and Reconstruction. 992 pp.*

Mannheim, Karl. Freedom, Power and Democratic Planning. *Edited by Hans Gerth and Ernest K. Bramstedt. 424 pp.*

Mansur, Fatma. Process of Independence. *Foreword by A. H. Hanson. 208 pp.*

Martin, David A. Pacificism: *an Historical and Sociological Study. 262 pp.*

Myrdal, Gunnar. The Political Element in the Development of Economic Theory. *Translated from the German by Paul Streeten. 282 pp.*

Wootton, Graham. Workers, Unions and the State. *188 pp.*

FOREIGN AFFAIRS: THEIR SOCIAL, POLITICAL AND ECONOMIC FOUNDATIONS

Mayer, J. P. Political Thought in France from the Revolution to the Fifth Republic. *164 pp.*

CRIMINOLOGY

Ancel, Marc. Social Defence: *A Modern Approach to Criminal Problems. Foreword by Leon Radzinowicz. 240 pp.*

Cloward, Richard A., and **Ohlin, Lloyd E.** Delinquency and Opportunity: *A Theory of Delinquent Gangs. 248 pp.*

Downes, David M. The Delinquent Solution. *A Study in Subcultural Theory. 296 pp.*

Dunlop, A. B., and **McCabe, S.** Young Men in Detention Centres. *192 pp.*

Friedlander, Kate. The Psycho-Analytical Approach to Juvenile Delinquency: *Theory, Case Studies, Treatment. 320 pp.*

Glueck, Sheldon, and **Eleanor.** Family Environment and Delinquency. *With the statistical assistance of Rose W. Kneznek. 340 pp.*

Lopez-Rey, Manuel. Crime. *An Analytical Appraisal. 288 pp.*

Mannheim, Hermann. Comparative Criminology: *a Text Book. Two volumes. 442 pp. and 380 pp.*

Morris, Terence. The Criminal Area: *A Study in Social Ecology. Foreword by Hermann Mannheim. 232 pp. 25 tables. 4 maps.*

● **Taylor, Ian, Walton, Paul,** and **Young, Jock.** The New Criminology. *For a Social Theory of Deviance.*

SOCIAL PSYCHOLOGY

Bagley, Christopher. The Social Psychology of the Epileptic Child. *320 pp.*

Barbu, Zevedei. Problems of Historical Psychology. *248 pp.*

Blackburn, Julian. Psychology and the Social Pattern. *184 pp.*

● **Brittan, Arthur.** Meanings and Situations. *224 pp.*

● **Fleming, C. M.** Adolescence: Its Social Psychology. *With an Introduction to recent findings from the fields of Anthropology, Physiology, Medicine, Psychometrics and Sociometry. 288 pp.*

● The Social Psychology of Education: *An Introduction and Guide to Its Study. 136 pp.*

Homans, George C. The Human Group. *Foreword by Bernard DeVoto. Introduction by Robert K. Merton. 526 pp.*

Social Behaviour: *its Elementary Forms. 416 pp.*

Klein, Josephine. The Study of Groups. *226 pp. 31 figures. 5 tables.*

Linton, Ralph. The Cultural Background of Personality. *132 pp.*

Mayo, Elton. The Social Problems of an Industrial Civilization. *With an appendix on the Political Problem. 180 pp.*

Ottaway, A. K. C. Learning Through Group Experience. *176 pp.*

Ridder, J. C. de. The Personality of the Urban African in South Africa. *A Thematic Apperception Test Study. 196 pp. 12 plates.*

● **Rose, Arnold M.** (Ed.). Human Behaviour and Social Processes: *an Interactionist Approach. Contributions by Arnold M. Rose, Ralph H. Turner, Anselm Strauss, Everett C. Hughes, E. Franklin Frazier, Howard S. Becker, et al. 696 pp.*

Smelser, Neil J. Theory of Collective Behaviour. *448 pp.*
Stephenson, Geoffrey M. The Development of Conscience. *128 pp.*
Young, Kimball. Handbook of Social Psychology. *658 pp. 16 figures. 10 tables.*

SOCIOLOGY OF THE FAMILY

Banks, J. A. Prosperity and Parenthood: *A Study of Family Planning among The Victorian Middle Classes. 262 pp.*
Bell, Colin R. Middle Class Families: *Social and Geographical Mobility. 224 pp.*
Burton, Lindy. Vulnerable Children. *272 pp.*
Gavron, Hannah. The Captive Wife: *Conflicts of Household Mothers. 190 pp.*
George, Victor, and **Wilding, Paul.** Motherless Families. *220 pp.*
Klein, Josephine. Samples from English Cultures.
   1. Three Preliminary Studies and Aspects of Adult Life in England. *447 pp.*
   2. Child-Rearing Practices and Index. *247 pp.*
Klein, Viola. Britain's Married Women Workers. *180 pp.*
   The Feminine Character. *History of an Ideology. 244 pp.*
McWhinnie, Alexina M. Adopted Children. *How They Grow Up. 304 pp.*
Myrdal, Alva, and **Klein, Viola.** Women's Two Roles: *Home and Work. 238 pp. 27 tables.*
Parsons, Talcott, and **Bales, Robert F.** Family: Socialization and Interaction Process. *In collaboration with James Olds, Morris Zelditch and Philip E. Slater. 456 pp. 50 figures and tables.*

SOCIAL SERVICES

Bastide, Roger. The Sociology of Mental Disorder. *Translated from the French by Jean McNeil. 260 pp.*
Carlebach, Julius. Caring For Children in Trouble. *266 pp.*
Forder, R. A. (Ed.). Penelope Hall's Social Services of England and Wales. *352 pp.*
George, Victor. Foster Care. *Theory and Practice. 234 pp.*
   Social Security: *Beveridge and After. 258 pp.*
● **Goetschius, George W.** Working with Community Groups. *256 pp.*
Goetschius, George W., and **Tash, Joan.** Working with Unattached Youth. *416 pp.*
Hall, M. P., and **Howes, I. V.** The Church in Social Work. *A Study of Moral Welfare Work undertaken by the Church of England. 320 pp.*
Heywood, Jean S. Children in Care: *the Development of the Service for the Deprived Child. 264 pp.*
Hoenig, J., and **Hamilton, Marian W.** The De-Segration of the Mentally Ill. *284 pp.*
Jones, Kathleen. Mental Health and Social Policy, 1845-1959. *264 pp.*

King, Roy D., Raynes, Norma V., and **Tizard, Jack.** Patterns of Residential Care. *356 pp.*

Leigh, John. Young People and Leisure. *256 pp.*

Morris, Mary. Voluntary Work and the Welfare State. *300 pp.*

Morris, Pauline. Put Away: *A Sociological Study of Institutions for the Mentally Retarded. 364 pp.*

Nokes, P. L. The Professional Task in Welfare Practice. *152 pp.*

Timms, Noel. Psychiatric Social Work in Great Britain (1939-1962). *280 pp.*
● Social Casework: *Principles and Practice. 256 pp.*

Young, A. F., and **Ashton, E. T.** British Social Work in the Nineteenth Century. *288 pp.*

Young, A. F. Social Services in British Industry. *272 pp.*

SOCIOLOGY OF EDUCATION

Banks, Olive. Parity and Prestige in English Secondary Education: a Study in Educational Sociology. *272 pp.*

Bentwich, Joseph. Education in Israel. *224 pp. 8 pp. plates.*

● **Blyth, W. A. L.** English Primary Education. *A Sociological Description.*
1. Schools. *232 pp.*
2. Background. *168 pp.*

Collier, K. G. The Social Purposes of Education: *Personal and Social Values in Education. 268 pp.*

Dale, R. R., and **Griffith, S.** Down Stream: *Failure in the Grammar School. 108 pp.*

Dore, R. P. Education in Tokugawa Japan. *356 pp. 9 pp. plates*

Evans, K. M. Sociometry and Education. *158 pp.*

Foster, P. J. Education and Social Change in Ghana. *336 pp. 3 maps.*

Fraser, W. R. Education and Society in Modern France. *150 pp.*

Grace, Gerald R. Role Conflict and the Teacher. *About 200 pp.*

Hans, Nicholas. New Trends in Education in the Eighteenth Century. *278 pp. 19 tables.*
● Comparative Education: *A Study of Educational Factors and Traditions. 360 pp.*

Hargreaves, David. Interpersonal Relations and Education. *432 pp.*
● Social Relations in a Secondary School. *240 pp.*

Holmes, Brian. Problems in Education. *A Comparative Approach. 336 pp.*

King, Ronald. Values and Involvement in a Grammar School. *164 pp.*
School Organization and Pupil Involvement. *A Study of Secondary Schools.*

● **Mannheim, Karl,** and **Stewart, W. A. C.** An Introduction to the Sociology of Education. *206 pp.*

Morris, Raymond N. The Sixth Form and College Entrance. *231 pp.*

● **Musgrove, F.** Youth and the Social Order. *176 pp.*

● **Ottaway, A. K. C.** Education and Society: An Introduction to the Sociology of Education. *With an Introduction by W. O. Lester Smith. 212 pp.*

Peers, Robert. Adult Education: *A Comparative Study. 398 pp.*

Pritchard, D. G. Education and the Handicapped: *1760 to 1960. 258 pp.*
Richardson, Helen. Adolescent Girls in Approved Schools. *308 pp.*
Stratta, Erica. The Education of Borstal Boys. *A Study of their Educational Experiences prior to, and during Borstal Training. 256 pp.*

SOCIOLOGY OF CULTURE

Eppel, E. M., and M. Adolescents and Morality: *A Study of some Moral Values and Dilemmas of Working Adolescents in the Context of a changing Climate of Opinion. Foreword by W. J. H. Sprott. 268 pp. 39 tables.*
● **Fromm, Erich.** The Fear of Freedom. *286 pp.*
The Sane Society. *400 pp.*
Mannheim, Karl. Essays on the Sociology of Culture. *Edited by Ernst Mannheim in co-operation with Paul Kecskemeti. Editorial Note by Adolph Lowe. 280 pp.*
Weber, Alfred. Farewell to European History: *or The Conquest of Nihilism Translated from the German by R. F. C. Hull. 224 pp.*

SOCIOLOGY OF RELIGION

Argyle, Michael. Religious Behaviour. *224 pp. 8 figures. 41 tables.*
Nelson, G. K. Spiritualism and Society. *313 pp.*
Stark, Werner. The Sociology of Religion. *A Study of Christendom.*
Volume I. *Established Religion. 248 pp.*
Volume II. *Sectarian Religion. 368 pp.*
Volume III. *The Universal Church. 464 pp.*
Volume IV. *Types of Religious Man. 352 pp.*
Volume V. *Types of Religious Culture. 464 pp.*
Watt, W. Montgomery. Islam and the Integration of Society. *320 pp.*

SOCIOLOGY OF ART AND LITERATURE

Jarvie, Ian C. Towards a Sociology of the Cinema. *A Comparative Essay on the Structure and Functioning of a Major Entertainment Industry. 405 pp.* •
Rust, Frances S. Dance in Society. *An Analysis of the Relationships between the Social Dance and Society in England from the Middle Ages to the Present Day. 256 pp. 8 pp. of plates.*
Schücking, L. L. The Sociology of Literary Taste. *112 pp.*

SOCIOLOGY OF KNOWLEDGE

Mannheim, Karl. Essays on the Sociology of Knowledge. *Edited by Paul Kecskemeti. Editorial Note by Adolph Lowe. 353 pp.*

Remmling, Gunter W. (Ed.). Towards the Sociology of Knowledge. *Origins and Development of a Sociological Thought Style.*

Stark, Werner. The Sociology of Knowledge: *An Essay in Aid of a Deeper Understanding of the History of Ideas. 384 pp.*

URBAN SOCIOLOGY

Ashworth, William. The Genesis of Modern British Town Planning: *A Study in Economic and Social History of the Nineteenth and Twentieth Centuries. 288 pp.*

Cullingworth, J. B. Housing Needs and Planning Policy: *A Restatement of the Problems of Housing Need and 'Overspill' in England and Wales. 232 pp. 44 tables. 8 maps.*

Dickinson, Robert E. City and Region: *A Geographical Interpretation. 608 pp. 125 figures.*

The West European City: *A Geographical Interpretation. 600 pp. 129 maps. 29 plates.*

● The City Region in Western Europe. *320 pp. Maps.*

Humphreys, Alexander J. New Dubliners: *Urbanization and the Irish Family. Foreword by George C. Homans. 304 pp.*

Jackson, Brian. Working Class Community: *Some General Notions raised by a Series of Studies in Northern England. 192 pp.*

Jennings, Hilda. Societies in the Making: *a Study of Development and Redevelopment within a County Borough. Foreword by D. A. Clark. 286 pp.*

● **Mann, P. H.** An Approach to Urban Sociology. *240 pp.*

Morris, R. N., and **Mogey, J.** The Sociology of Housing. *Studies at Berinsfield. 232 pp. 4 pp. plates.*

Rosser, C., and **Harris, C.** The Family and Social Change. *A Study of Family and Kinship in a South Wales Town. 352 pp. 8 maps.*

RURAL SOCIOLOGY

Chambers, R. J. H. Settlement Schemes in Tropical Africa: *A Selective Study. 268 pp.*

Haswell, M. R. The Economics of Development in Village India. *120 pp.*

Littlejohn, James. Westrigg: *the Sociology of a Cheviot Parish. 172 pp. 5 figures.*

Mayer, Adrian C. Peasants in the Pacific. *A Study of Fiji Indian Rural Society. 248 pp. 20 plates.*

Williams, W. M. The Sociology of an English Village: *Gosforth. 272 pp. 12 figures. 13 tables.*

SOCIOLOGY OF INDUSTRY AND DISTRIBUTION

Anderson, Nels. Work and Leisure. *280 pp.*

● **Blau, Peter M.**, and **Scott, W. Richard.** Formal Organizations: *a Comparative approach. Introduction and Additional Bibliography by J. H. Smith. 326 pp.*

Eldridge, J. E. T. Industrial Disputes. *Essays in the Sociology of Industrial Relations. 288 pp.*

Hetzler, Stanley. Applied Measures for Promoting Technological Growth. *352 pp.*

Technological Growth and Social Change. *Achieving Modernization. 269 pp.*

Hollowell, Peter G. The Lorry Driver. *272 pp.*

Jefferys, Margot, *with the assistance of Winifred Moss.* Mobility in the Labour Market: *Employment Changes in Battersea and Dagenham. Preface by Barbara Wootton. 186 pp. 51 tables.*

Millerson, Geoffrey. The Qualifying Associations: *a Study in Professionalization. 320 pp.*

Smelser, Neil J. Social Change in the Industrial Revolution: *An Application of Theory to the Lancashire Cotton Industry, 1770-1840. 468 pp. 12 figures. 14 tables.*

Williams, Gertrude. Recruitment to Skilled Trades. *240 pp.*

Young, A. F. Industrial Injuries Insurance: *an Examination of British Policy. 192 pp.*

DOCUMENTARY

Schlesinger, Rudolf (Ed.). Changing Attitudes in Soviet Russia.
2. The Nationalities Problem and Soviet Administration. *Selected Readings on the Development of Soviet Nationalities Policies. Introduced by the editor. Translated by W. W. Gottlieb. 324 pp.*

ANTHROPOLOGY

Ammar, Hamed. Growing up in an Egyptian Village: *Silwa, Province of Aswan. 336 pp.*

Brandel-Syrier, Mia. Reeftown Elite. *A Study of Social Mobility in a Modern African Community on the Reef. 376 pp.*

Crook, David, and **Isabel.** Revolution in a Chinese Village: *Ten Mile Inn. 230 pp. 8 plates. 1 map.*

Dickie-Clark, H. F. The Marginal Situation. *A Sociological Study of a Coloured Group. 236 pp.*

Dube, S. C. Indian Village. *Foreword by Morris Edward Opler. 276 pp. 4 plates.*

India's Changing Villages: *Human Factors in Community Development. 260 pp. 8 plates. 1 map.*

Firth, Raymond. Malay Fishermen. *Their Peasant Economy. 420 pp. 17 pp. plates.*

Gulliver, P. H. Social Control in an African Society: a Study of the Arusha, Agricultural Masai of Northern Tanganyika. *320 pp. 8 plates. 10 figures.*

Ishwaran, K. Shivapur. *A South Indian Village. 216 pp.*
Tradition and Economy in Village India: *An Interactionist Approach. Foreword by Conrad Arensburg. 176 pp.*

Jarvie, Ian C. The Revolution in Anthropology. *268 pp.*

Jarvie, Ian C., and **Agassi, Joseph.** Hong Kong. *A Society in Transition. 396 pp. Illustrated with plates and maps.*

Little, Kenneth L. Mende of Sierra Leone. *308 pp. and folder.*
Negroes in Britain. *With a New Introduction and Contemporary Study by Leonard Bloom. 320 pp.*

Lowie, Robert H. Social Organization. *494 pp.*

Mayer, Adrian C. Caste and Kinship in Central India: *A Village and its Region. 328 pp. 16 plates. 15 figures. 16 tables.*

Smith, Raymond T. The Negro Family in British Guiana: *Family Structure and Social Status in the Villages. With a Foreword by Meyer Fortes. 314 pp. 8 plates. 1 figure. 4 maps.*

SOCIOLOGY AND PHILOSOPHY

Barnsley, John H. The Social Reality of Ethics. *A Comparative Analysis of Moral Codes. 448 pp.*

Diesing, Paul. Patterns of Discovery in the Social Sciences. *362 pp.*

Douglas, Jack D. (Ed.). Understanding Everyday Life. *Toward the Reconstruction of Sociological Knowledge. Contributions by Alan F. Blum. Aaron W. Cicourel, Norman K. Denzin, Jack D. Douglas, John Heeren, Peter McHugh, Peter K. Manning, Melvin Power, Matthew Speier, Roy Turner, D. Lawrence Wieder, Thomas P. Wilson and Don H. Zimmerman. 370 pp.*

Jarvie, Ian C. Concepts and Society. *216 pp.*

Roche, Maurice. Phenomenology, Language and the Social Sciences. *About 400 pp.*

Sahay, Arun. Sociological Analysis.

Sklair, Leslie. The Sociology of Progress. *320 pp.*

International Library of Anthropology
General Editor Adam Kuper

Brown, Paula. The Chimbu. *A Study of Change in the New Guinea Highlands.*
Van Den Berghe, Pierre L. Power and Privilege at an African University.

International Library
of Social Policy
General Editor   Kathleen Jones

Holman, Robert. Trading in Children. *A Study of Private Fostering.*
Jones, Kathleen. History of the Mental Health Services. *428 pp.*
Thomas, J. E. The English Prison Officer since 1850: *A Study in Conflict.*
  258 pp.

Primary Socialization, Language
and Education
General Editor   Basil Bernstein

Bernstein, Basil. Class, Codes and Control. *2 volumes.*
  1. *Theoretical Studies Towards a Sociology of Language. 254 pp.*
  2. *Applied Studies Towards a Sociology of Language. About 400 pp.*
Brandis, Walter, and **Henderson, Dorothy.** Social Class, Language and
  Communication. *288 pp.*
Cook-Gumperz, Jenny. Social Control and Socialization. *A Study of Class
  Differences in the Language of Maternal Control.*
Gahagan, D. M., and **G. A.** Talk Reform. *Exploration in Language for Infant
  School Children. 160 pp.*
Robinson, W. P., and **Rackstraw, Susan, D. A.** A Question of Answers.
  2 volumes. 192 pp. and 180 pp.
Turner, Geoffrey, J., and **Mohan, Bernard, A.** A Linguistic Description and
  Computer Programme for Children's Speech. *208 pp.*

Reports of the Institute of Community Studies

Cartwright, Ann. Human Relations and Hospital Care. *272 pp.*
  Parents and Family Planning Services. *306 pp.*
  Patients and their Doctors. *A Study of General Practice. 304 pp.*
● **Jackson, Brian.** Streaming: *an Education System in Miniature. 168 pp.*
Jackson, Brian, and **Marsden, Dennis.** Education and the Working Class:
  *Some General Themes raised by a Study of 88 Working-class Children
  in a Northern Industrial City. 268 pp. 2 folders.*
Marris, Peter. The Experience of Higher Education. *232 pp. 27 tables.*
Marris, Peter, and **Rein, Martin.** Dilemmas of Social Reform. *Poverty and
  Community Action in the United States. 256 pp.*
Marris, Peter, and **Somerset, Anthony.** African Businessmen. *A Study of
  Entrepreneurship and Development in Kenya. 256 pp.*
Mills, Richard. Young Outsiders: *a Study in Alternative Communities.*

Runciman, W. G. Relative Deprivation and Social Justice. *A Study of Attitudes to Social Inequality in Twentieth Century England. 352 pp.*

Townsend, Peter. The Family Life of Old People: *An Inquiry in East London. Foreword by J. H. Sheldon. 300 pp. 3 figures. 63 tables.*

Willmott, Peter. Adolescent Boys in East London. *230 pp.*
The Evolution of a Community: *a study of Dagenham after forty years. 168 pp. 2 maps.*

Willmott, Peter, and **Young, Michael.** Family and Class in a London Suburb. *202 pp. 47 tables.*

Young, Michael. Innovation and Research in Education. *192 pp.*

● **Young, Michael,** and **McGeeney, Patrick.** Learning Begins at Home. *A Study of a Junior School and its Parents. 128 pp.*

Young, Michael, and **Willmott, Peter.** Family and Kinship in East London. *Foreword by Richard M. Titmuss. 252 pp. 39 tables.*
The Symmetrical Family.

Reports of the Institute for Social Studies in Medical Care

Cartwright, Ann, Hockey, Lisbeth, and **Anderson, John L.** Life Before Death.

Dunnell, Karen, and **Cartwright, Ann.** Medicine Takers, Prescribers and Hoarders. *190 pp.*

Medicine, Illness and Society
General Editor W. M. Williams

Robinson, David. The Process of Becoming Ill.

Stacey, Margaret. *et al.* Hospitals, Children and Their Families. *The Report of a Pilot Study. 202 pp.*

Monographs in Social Theory
General Editor Arthur Brittan

Bauman, Zygmunt. Culture as Praxis.

Dixon, Keith. Sociological Theory. *Pretence and Possibility.*

Smith, Anthony D. The Concept of Social Change. *A Critique of the Functionalist Theory of Social Change.*

Routledge Social Science Journals

The British Journal of Sociology. *Edited by Terence P. Morris. Vol. 1, No. 1, March 1950 and Quarterly. Roy. 8vo. Back numbers available. An international journal with articles on all aspects of sociology.*

Economy and Society. *Vol. 1, No. 1. February 1972 and Quarterly. Metric Roy. 8vo. A journal for all social scientists covering sociology, philosophy, anthropology, economics and history. Back numbers available.*

Year Book of Social Policy in Britain, The. *Edited by Kathleen Jones. 1971. Published Annually.*

Printed in Great Britain by Lewis Reprints Limited
Brown Knight & Truscott Group, London and Tonbridge

1373

14